Mometrix
TEST PREPARATION

I0878900

Series 27
Exam Secrets Study Guide

Dear Future Exam Success Story

First of all, **THANK YOU** for purchasing Mometrix study materials!

Second, congratulations! You are one of the few determined test-takers who are committed to doing whatever it takes to excel on your exam. **You have come to the right place.** We developed these study materials with one goal in mind: to deliver you the information you need in a format that's concise and easy to use.

In addition to optimizing your guide for the content of the test, we've outlined our recommended steps for breaking down the preparation process into small, attainable goals so you can make sure you stay on track.

We've also analyzed the entire test-taking process, identifying the most common pitfalls and showing how you can overcome them and be ready for any curveball the test throws you.

Standardized testing is one of the biggest obstacles on your road to success, which only increases the importance of doing well in the high-pressure, high-stakes environment of test day. Your results on this test could have a significant impact on your future, and this guide provides the information and practical advice to help you achieve your full potential on test day.

Your success is our success

We would love to hear from you! If you would like to share the story of your exam success or if you have any questions or comments in regard to our products, please contact us at **800-673-8175** or **support@mometrix.com**.

Thanks again for your business and we wish you continued success!

Sincerely,
The Mometrix Test Preparation Team

Need more help? Check out our flashcards at:
http://MometrixFlashcards.com/Series27

Written and edited by the Mometrix Exam Secrets Test Prep Team
Printed in the United States of America

Table of Contents

Introduction

Thank you for purchasing this resource! You have made the choice to prepare yourself for a test that could have a huge impact on your future, and this guide is designed to help you be fully ready for test day. Obviously, it's important to have a solid understanding of the test material, but you also need to be prepared for the unique environment and stressors of the test, so that you can perform to the best of your abilities.

For this purpose, the first section that appears in this guide is the **Secret Keys**. We've devoted countless hours to meticulously researching what works and what doesn't, and we've boiled down our findings to the five most impactful steps you can take to improve your performance on the test. We start at the beginning with study planning and move through the preparation process, all the way to the testing strategies that will help you get the most out of what you know when you're finally sitting in front of the test.

We recommend that you start preparing for your test as far in advance as possible. However, if you've bought this guide as a last-minute study resource and only have a few days before your test, we recommend that you skip over the first two Secret Keys since they address a long-term study plan.

If you struggle with **test anxiety**, we strongly encourage you to check out our recommendations for how you can overcome it. Test anxiety is a formidable foe, but it can be beaten, and we want to make sure you have the tools you need to defeat it.

Secret Key 1: Plan Big, Study Small

There's a lot riding on your performance. If you want to ace this test, you're going to need to keep your skills sharp and the material fresh in your mind. You need a plan that lets you review everything you need to know while still fitting in your schedule. We'll break this strategy down into three categories.

Information Organization

Start with the information you already have: the official test outline. From this, you can make a complete list of all the concepts you need to cover before the test. Organize these concepts into groups that can be studied together, and create a list of any related vocabulary you need to learn so you can brush up on any difficult terms. You'll want to keep this vocabulary list handy once you actually start studying since you may need to add to it along the way.

Time Management

Once you have your set of study concepts, decide how to spread them out over the time you have left before the test. Break your study plan into small, clear goals so you have a manageable task for each day and know exactly what you're doing. Then just focus on one small step at a time. When you manage your time this way, you don't need to spend hours at a time studying. Studying a small block of content for a short period each day helps you retain information better and avoid stressing over how much you have left to do. You can relax knowing that you have a plan to cover everything in time. In order for this strategy to be effective though, you have to start studying early and stick to your schedule. Avoid the exhaustion and futility that comes from last-minute cramming!

Study Environment

The environment you study in has a big impact on your learning. Studying in a coffee shop, while probably more enjoyable, is not likely to be as fruitful as studying in a quiet room. It's important to keep distractions to a minimum. You're only planning to study for a short block of time, so make the most of it. Don't pause to check your phone or get up to find a snack. It's also important to **avoid multitasking**. Research has consistently shown that multitasking will make your studying dramatically less effective. Your study area should also be comfortable and well-lit so you don't have the distraction of straining your eyes or sitting on an uncomfortable chair.

The time of day you study is also important. You want to be rested and alert. Don't wait until just before bedtime. Study when you'll be most likely to comprehend and remember. Even better, if you know what time of day your test will be, set that time aside for study. That way your brain will be used to working on that subject at that specific time and you'll have a better chance of recalling information.

Finally, it can be helpful to team up with others who are studying for the same test. Your actual studying should be done in as isolated an environment as possible, but the work of organizing the information and setting up the study plan can be divided up. In between study sessions, you can discuss with your teammates the concepts that you're all studying and quiz each other on the details. Just be sure that your teammates are as serious about the test as you are. If you find that your study time is being replaced with social time, you might need to find a new team.

Secret Key 2: Make Your Studying Count

You're devoting a lot of time and effort to preparing for this test, so you want to be absolutely certain it will pay off. This means doing more than just reading the content and hoping you can remember it on test day. It's important to make every minute of study count. There are two main areas you can focus on to make your studying count.

Retention

It doesn't matter how much time you study if you can't remember the material. You need to make sure you are retaining the concepts. To check your retention of the information you're learning, try recalling it at later times with minimal prompting. Try carrying around flashcards and glance at one or two from time to time or ask a friend who's also studying for the test to quiz you.

To enhance your retention, look for ways to put the information into practice so that you can apply it rather than simply recalling it. If you're using the information in practical ways, it will be much easier to remember. Similarly, it helps to solidify a concept in your mind if you're not only reading it to yourself but also explaining it to someone else. Ask a friend to let you teach them about a concept you're a little shaky on (or speak aloud to an imaginary audience if necessary). As you try to summarize, define, give examples, and answer your friend's questions, you'll understand the concepts better and they will stay with you longer. Finally, step back for a big picture view and ask yourself how each piece of information fits with the whole subject. When you link the different concepts together and see them working together as a whole, it's easier to remember the individual components.

Finally, practice showing your work on any multi-step problems, even if you're just studying. Writing out each step you take to solve a problem will help solidify the process in your mind, and you'll be more likely to remember it during the test.

Modality

Modality simply refers to the means or method by which you study. Choosing a study modality that fits your own individual learning style is crucial. No two people learn best in exactly the same way, so it's important to know your strengths and use them to your advantage.

For example, if you learn best by visualization, focus on visualizing a concept in your mind and draw an image or a diagram. Try color-coding your notes, illustrating them, or creating symbols that will trigger your mind to recall a learned concept. If you learn best by hearing or discussing information, find a study partner who learns the same way or read aloud to yourself. Think about how to put the information in your own words. Imagine that you are giving a lecture on the topic and record yourself so you can listen to it later.

For any learning style, flashcards can be helpful. Organize the information so you can take advantage of spare moments to review. Underline key words or phrases. Use different colors for different categories. Mnemonic devices (such as creating a short list in which every item starts with the same letter) can also help with retention. Find what works best for you and use it to store the information in your mind most effectively and easily.

Secret Key 3: Practice the Right Way

Your success on test day depends not only on how many hours you put into preparing, but also on whether you prepared the right way. It's good to check along the way to see if your studying is paying off. One of the most effective ways to do this is by taking practice tests to evaluate your progress. Practice tests are useful because they show exactly where you need to improve. Every time you take a practice test, pay special attention to these three groups of questions:

- The questions you got wrong
- The questions you had to guess on, even if you guessed right
- The questions you found difficult or slow to work through

This will show you exactly what your weak areas are, and where you need to devote more study time. Ask yourself why each of these questions gave you trouble. Was it because you didn't understand the material? Was it because you didn't remember the vocabulary? Do you need more repetitions on this type of question to build speed and confidence? Dig into those questions and figure out how you can strengthen your weak areas as you go back to review the material.

Additionally, many practice tests have a section explaining the answer choices. It can be tempting to read the explanation and think that you now have a good understanding of the concept. However, an explanation likely only covers part of the question's broader context. Even if the explanation makes perfect sense, **go back and investigate** every concept related to the question until you're positive you have a thorough understanding.

As you go along, keep in mind that the practice test is just that: practice. Memorizing these questions and answers will not be very helpful on the actual test because it is unlikely to have any of the same exact questions. If you only know the right answers to the sample questions, you won't be prepared for the real thing. **Study the concepts** until you understand them fully, and then you'll be able to answer any question that shows up on the test.

It's important to wait on the practice tests until you're ready. If you take a test on your first day of study, you may be overwhelmed by the amount of material covered and how much you need to learn. Work up to it gradually.

On test day, you'll need to be prepared for answering questions, managing your time, and using the test-taking strategies you've learned. It's a lot to balance, like a mental marathon that will have a big impact on your future. Like training for a marathon, you'll need to start slowly and work your way up. When test day arrives, you'll be ready.

Start with the strategies you've read in the first two Secret Keys—plan your course and study in the way that works best for you. If you have time, consider using multiple study resources to get different approaches to the same concepts. It can be helpful to see difficult concepts from more than one angle. Then find a good source for practice tests. Many times, the test website will suggest potential study resources or provide sample tests.

Practice Test Strategy

If you're able to find at least three practice tests, we recommend this strategy:

Untimed and Open-Book Practice

Take the first test with no time constraints and with your notes and study guide handy. Take your time and focus on applying the strategies you've learned.

Timed and Open-Book Practice

Take the second practice test open-book as well, but set a timer and practice pacing yourself to finish in time.

Timed and Closed-Book Practice

Take any other practice tests as if it were test day. Set a timer and put away your study materials. Sit at a table or desk in a quiet room, imagine yourself at the testing center, and answer questions as quickly and accurately as possible.

Keep repeating timed and closed-book tests on a regular basis until you run out of practice tests or it's time for the actual test. Your mind will be ready for the schedule and stress of test day, and you'll be able to focus on recalling the material you've learned.

Secret Key 4: Pace Yourself

Once you're fully prepared for the material on the test, your biggest challenge on test day will be managing your time. Just knowing that the clock is ticking can make you panic even if you have plenty of time left. Work on pacing yourself so you can build confidence against the time constraints of the exam. Pacing is a difficult skill to master, especially in a high-pressure environment, so **practice is vital**.

Set time expectations for your pace based on how much time is available. For example, if a section has 60 questions and the time limit is 30 minutes, you know you have to average 30 seconds or less per question in order to answer them all. Although 30 seconds is the hard limit, set 25 seconds per question as your goal, so you reserve extra time to spend on harder questions. When you budget extra time for the harder questions, you no longer have any reason to stress when those questions take longer to answer.

Don't let this time expectation distract you from working through the test at a calm, steady pace, but keep it in mind so you don't spend too much time on any one question. Recognize that taking extra time on one question you don't understand may keep you from answering two that you do understand later in the test. If your time limit for a question is up and you're still not sure of the answer, mark it and move on, and come back to it later if the time and the test format allow. If the testing format doesn't allow you to return to earlier questions, just make an educated guess; then put it out of your mind and move on.

On the easier questions, be careful not to rush. It may seem wise to hurry through them so you have more time for the challenging ones, but it's not worth missing one if you know the concept and just didn't take the time to read the question fully. Work efficiently but make sure you understand the question and have looked at all of the answer choices, since more than one may seem right at first.

Even if you're paying attention to the time, you may find yourself a little behind at some point. You should speed up to get back on track, but do so wisely. Don't panic; just take a few seconds less on each question until you're caught up. Don't guess without thinking, but do look through the answer choices and eliminate any you know are wrong. If you can get down to two choices, it is often worthwhile to guess from those. Once you've chosen an answer, move on and don't dwell on any that you skipped or had to hurry through. If a question was taking too long, chances are it was one of the harder ones, so you weren't as likely to get it right anyway.

On the other hand, if you find yourself getting ahead of schedule, it may be beneficial to slow down a little. The more quickly you work, the more likely you are to make a careless mistake that will affect your score. You've budgeted time for each question, so don't be afraid to spend that time. Practice an efficient but careful pace to get the most out of the time you have.

Secret Key 5: Have a Plan for Guessing

When you're taking the test, you may find yourself stuck on a question. Some of the answer choices seem better than others, but you don't see the one answer choice that is obviously correct. What do you do?

The scenario described above is very common, yet most test takers have not effectively prepared for it. Developing and practicing a plan for guessing may be one of the single most effective uses of your time as you get ready for the exam.

In developing your plan for guessing, there are three questions to address:

- When should you start the guessing process?
- How should you narrow down the choices?
- Which answer should you choose?

When to Start the Guessing Process

Unless your plan for guessing is to select C every time (which, despite its merits, is not what we recommend), you need to leave yourself enough time to apply your answer elimination strategies. Since you have a limited amount of time for each question, that means that if you're going to give yourself the best shot at guessing correctly, you have to decide quickly whether or not you will guess.

Of course, the best-case scenario is that you don't have to guess at all, so first, see if you can answer the question based on your knowledge of the subject and basic reasoning skills. Focus on the key words in the question and try to jog your memory of related topics. Give yourself a chance to bring the knowledge to mind, but once you realize that you don't have (or you can't access) the knowledge you need to answer the question, it's time to start the guessing process.

It's almost always better to start the guessing process too early than too late. It only takes a few seconds to remember something and answer the question from knowledge. Carefully eliminating wrong answer choices takes longer. Plus, going through the process of eliminating answer choices can actually help jog your memory.

Summary: Start the guessing process as soon as you decide that you can't answer the question based on your knowledge.

How to Narrow Down the Choices

The next chapter in this book (**Test-Taking Strategies**) includes a wide range of strategies for how to approach questions and how to look for answer choices to eliminate. You will definitely want to read those carefully, practice them, and figure out which ones work best for you. Here though, we're going to address a mindset rather than a particular strategy.

Your odds of guessing an answer correctly depend on how many options you are choosing from.

Number of options left	5	4	3	2	1
Odds of guessing correctly	20%	25%	33%	50%	100%

You can see from this chart just how valuable it is to be able to eliminate incorrect answers and make an educated guess, but there are two things that many test takers do that cause them to miss out on the benefits of guessing:

- Accidentally eliminating the correct answer
- Selecting an answer based on an impression

We'll look at the first one here, and the second one in the next section.

To avoid accidentally eliminating the correct answer, we recommend a thought exercise called **the $5 challenge**. In this challenge, you only eliminate an answer choice from contention if you are willing to bet $5 on it being wrong. Why $5? Five dollars is a small but not insignificant amount of money. It's an amount you could afford to lose but wouldn't want to throw away. And while losing $5 once might not hurt too much, doing it twenty times will set you back $100. In the same way, each small decision you make—eliminating a choice here, guessing on a question there—won't by itself impact your score very much, but when you put them all together, they can make a big difference. By holding each answer choice elimination decision to a higher standard, you can reduce the risk of accidentally eliminating the correct answer.

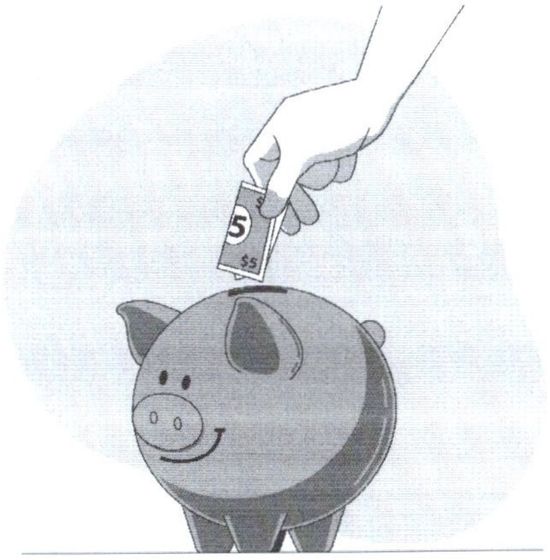

The $5 challenge can also be applied in a positive sense: If you are willing to bet $5 that an answer choice *is* correct, go ahead and mark it as correct.

Summary: Only eliminate an answer choice if you are willing to bet $5 that it is wrong.

Which Answer to Choose

You're taking the test. You've run into a hard question and decided you'll have to guess. You've eliminated all the answer choices you're willing to bet $5 on. Now you have to pick an answer. Why do we even need to talk about this? Why can't you just pick whichever one you feel like when the time comes?

The answer to these questions is that if you don't come into the test with a plan, you'll rely on your impression to select an answer choice, and if you do that, you risk falling into a trap. The test writers know that everyone who takes their test will be guessing on some of the questions, so they intentionally write wrong answer choices to seem plausible. You still have to pick an answer though, and if the wrong answer choices are designed to look right, how can you ever be sure that you're not falling for their trap? The best solution we've found to this dilemma is to take the decision out of your hands entirely. Here is the process we recommend:

Once you've eliminated any choices that you are confident (willing to bet $5) are wrong, select the first remaining choice as your answer.

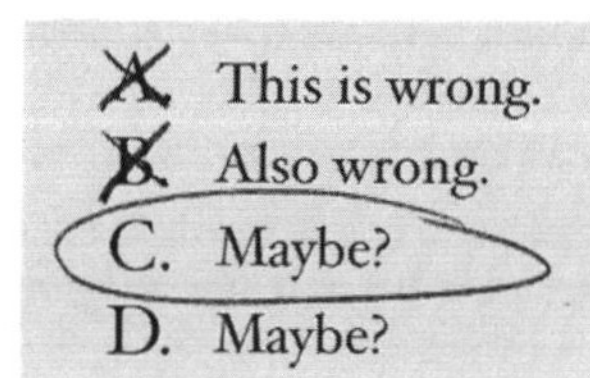

Whether you choose to select the first remaining choice, the second, or the last, the important thing is that you use some preselected standard. Using this approach guarantees that you will not be enticed into selecting an answer choice that looks right, because you are not basing your decision on how the answer choices look.

This is not meant to make you question your knowledge. Instead, it is to help you recognize the difference between your knowledge and your impressions. There's a huge difference between thinking an answer is right because of what you know, and thinking an answer is right because it looks or sounds like it should be right.

Summary: To ensure that your selection is appropriately random, make a predetermined selection from among all answer choices you have not eliminated.

Test-Taking Strategies

This section contains a list of test-taking strategies that you may find helpful as you work through the test. By taking what you know and applying logical thought, you can maximize your chances of answering any question correctly!

It is very important to realize that every question is different and every person is different: no single strategy will work on every question, and no single strategy will work for every person. That's why we've included all of them here, so you can try them out and determine which ones work best for different types of questions and which ones work best for you.

Question Strategies

✓ Read Carefully

Read the question and the answer choices carefully. Don't miss the question because you misread the terms. You have plenty of time to read each question thoroughly and make sure you understand what is being asked. Yet a happy medium must be attained, so don't waste too much time. You must read carefully and efficiently.

✓ Contextual Clues

Look for contextual clues. If the question includes a word you are not familiar with, look at the immediate context for some indication of what the word might mean. Contextual clues can often give you all the information you need to decipher the meaning of an unfamiliar word. Even if you can't determine the meaning, you may be able to narrow down the possibilities enough to make a solid guess at the answer to the question.

✓ Prefixes

If you're having trouble with a word in the question or answer choices, try dissecting it. Take advantage of every clue that the word might include. Prefixes can be a huge help. Usually, they allow you to determine a basic meaning. *Pre-* means before, *post-* means after, *pro-* is positive, *de-* is negative. From prefixes, you can get an idea of the general meaning of the word and try to put it into context.

✓ Hedge Words

Watch out for critical hedge words, such as *likely, may, can, often, almost, mostly, usually, generally, rarely,* and *sometimes.* Question writers insert these hedge phrases to cover every possibility. Often an answer choice will be wrong simply because it leaves no room for exception. Be on guard for answer choices that have definitive words such as *exactly* and *always.*

✓ Switchback Words

Stay alert for *switchbacks*. These are the words and phrases frequently used to alert you to shifts in thought. The most common switchback words are *but*, *although*, and *however*. Others include *nevertheless*, *on the other hand*, *even though*, *while*, *in spite of*, *despite*, and *regardless of*. Switchback words are important to catch because they can change the direction of the question or an answer choice.

✓ Face Value

When in doubt, use common sense. Accept the situation in the problem at face value. Don't read too much into it. These problems will not require you to make wild assumptions. If you have to go beyond creativity and warp time or space in order to have an answer choice fit the question, then you should move on and consider the other answer choices. These are normal problems rooted in reality. The applicable relationship or explanation may not be readily apparent, but it is there for you to figure out. Use your common sense to interpret anything that isn't clear.

Answer Choice Strategies

✓ Answer Selection

The most thorough way to pick an answer choice is to identify and eliminate wrong answers until only one is left, then confirm it is the correct answer. Sometimes an answer choice may immediately seem right, but be careful. The test writers will usually put more than one reasonable answer choice on each question, so take a second to read all of them and make sure that the other choices are not equally obvious. As long as you have time left, it is better to read every answer choice than to pick the first one that looks right without checking the others.

✓ Answer Choice Families

An answer choice family consists of two (in rare cases, three) answer choices that are very similar in construction and cannot all be true at the same time. If you see two answer choices that are direct opposites or parallels, one of them is usually the correct answer. For instance, if one answer choice says that quantity x increases and another either says that quantity x decreases (opposite) or says that quantity y increases (parallel), then those answer choices would fall into the same family. An answer choice that doesn't match the construction of the answer choice family is more likely to be incorrect. Most questions will not have answer choice families, but when they do appear, you should be prepared to recognize them.

✓ Eliminate Answers

Eliminate answer choices as soon as you realize they are wrong, but make sure you consider all possibilities. If you are eliminating answer choices and realize that the last one you are left with is also wrong, don't panic. Start over and consider each choice again. There may be something you missed the first time that you will realize on the second pass.

☑ Avoid Fact Traps

Don't be distracted by an answer choice that is factually true but doesn't answer the question. You are looking for the choice that answers the question. Stay focused on what the question is asking for so you don't accidentally pick an answer that is true but incorrect. Always go back to the question and make sure the answer choice you've selected actually answers the question and is not merely a true statement.

☑ Extreme Statements

In general, you should avoid answers that put forth extreme actions as standard practice or proclaim controversial ideas as established fact. An answer choice that states the "process should be used in certain situations, if…" is much more likely to be correct than one that states the "process should be discontinued completely." The first is a calm rational statement and doesn't even make a definitive, uncompromising stance, using a hedge word *if* to provide wiggle room, whereas the second choice is far more extreme.

☑ Benchmark

As you read through the answer choices and you come across one that seems to answer the question well, mentally select that answer choice. This is not your final answer, but it's the one that will help you evaluate the other answer choices. The one that you selected is your benchmark or standard for judging each of the other answer choices. Every other answer choice must be compared to your benchmark. That choice is correct until proven otherwise by another answer choice beating it. If you find a better answer, then that one becomes your new benchmark. Once you've decided that no other choice answers the question as well as your benchmark, you have your final answer.

☑ Predict the Answer

Before you even start looking at the answer choices, it is often best to try to predict the answer. When you come up with the answer on your own, it is easier to avoid distractions and traps because you will know exactly what to look for. The right answer choice is unlikely to be word-for-word what you came up with, but it should be a close match. Even if you are confident that you have the right answer, you should still take the time to read each option before moving on.

General Strategies

☑ Tough Questions

If you are stumped on a problem or it appears too hard or too difficult, don't waste time. Move on! Remember though, if you can quickly check for obviously incorrect answer choices, your chances of guessing correctly are greatly improved. Before you completely give up, at least try to knock out a couple of possible answers. Eliminate what you can and then guess at the remaining answer choices before moving on.

⊘ CHECK YOUR WORK

Since you will probably not know every term listed and the answer to every question, it is important that you get credit for the ones that you do know. Don't miss any questions through careless mistakes. If at all possible, try to take a second to look back over your answer selection and make sure you've selected the correct answer choice and haven't made a costly careless mistake (such as marking an answer choice that you didn't mean to mark). This quick double check should more than pay for itself in caught mistakes for the time it costs.

⊘ PACE YOURSELF

It's easy to be overwhelmed when you're looking at a page full of questions; your mind is confused and full of random thoughts, and the clock is ticking down faster than you would like. Calm down and maintain the pace that you have set for yourself. Especially as you get down to the last few minutes of the test, don't let the small numbers on the clock make you panic. As long as you are on track by monitoring your pace, you are guaranteed to have time for each question.

⊘ DON'T RUSH

It is very easy to make errors when you are in a hurry. Maintaining a fast pace in answering questions is pointless if it makes you miss questions that you would have gotten right otherwise. Test writers like to include distracting information and wrong answers that seem right. Taking a little extra time to avoid careless mistakes can make all the difference in your test score. Find a pace that allows you to be confident in the answers that you select.

⊘ KEEP MOVING

Panicking will not help you pass the test, so do your best to stay calm and keep moving. Taking deep breaths and going through the answer elimination steps you practiced can help to break through a stress barrier and keep your pace.

Final Notes

The combination of a solid foundation of content knowledge and the confidence that comes from practicing your plan for applying that knowledge is the key to maximizing your performance on test day. As your foundation of content knowledge is built up and strengthened, you'll find that the strategies included in this chapter become more and more effective in helping you quickly sift through the distractions and traps of the test to isolate the correct answer.

Now that you're preparing to move forward into the test content chapters of this book, be sure to keep your goal in mind. As you read, think about how you will be able to apply this information on the test. If you've already seen sample questions for the test and you have an idea of the question format and style, try to come up with questions of your own that you can answer based on what you're reading. This will give you valuable practice applying your knowledge in the same ways you can expect to on test day.

Good luck and good studying!

Keeping and Preservation of Records and Broker-dealer Requirements

When, As, and If Issued Contracts

Uniform Practice Code (UPC) Rule 11130 states that each party to a transaction must send written confirmation or comparisons and that they must be in the same uniform format. Each confirmation and comparison for When, As, and If Issued Contracts must contain at a minimum the following:

1. An adequate description of the security and the plan—this can be provided by the Security & Exchange Commission (SEC) if desired
2. Designation as a Financial Industry Regulatory Authority (FINRA) as the ruling authority
3. Provision for marking the contract to market
4. Whether the contract is trading flat or with accrued interest

Records That a Broker–Dealer Is Required to Keep Related to Customer Transactions

The first record is a blotter, which must be created daily and provides detail for all purchases and sales, deliveries of securities, and receipts of cash that occurred that day. The details must include the following:

1. The account in which the transaction occurred
2. The name and amount of securities
3. The per-unit and aggregate purchase or sale price
4. The trade date
5. The name of the person who sold the securities
6. The name of the person who received the securities

The second record is a ledger that should include the following details:

1. All assets and liabilities: this includes both liquid and illiquid assets along with long-term and short-term liabilities
2. All income and expenses: this should be current income kept on a cash basis
3. All capital accounts: any account that tracks the movement of funds for both investments and debts

The third record is a ledger that will help ensure that transactions are appropriately credited the right account and determine whether margin calls are required. The ledger should include the following details:

1. Cash and margin account information for each customer kept on a per-account basis
2. All purchases, sales, receipts, and deliveries for each customer account
3. All debits and credits to each customer account

The fourth record is a ledger that allows the broker to determine exactly where each security is located. This ledger should include the following details:

1. Securities in transfer (both awaiting transfer and awaiting delivery)
2. Dividends received
3. Interest received
4. Securities borrowed
5. Securities loaned
6. Securities failed to receive
7. Securities failed to deliver
8. Any record differences between what an examination shows an account should hold versus the recorded amount
9. Repurchase and reverse repurchase agreements

The fifth record is a securities record that should include the following details:

1. All long positions carried by the member on behalf of a customer, including the location of the securities and any recorded differences between the number of shares in the account and the number the account should hold
2. All short positions carried by the member on behalf a customer, including the location of the securities and any recorded differences between the number of shares in the account and the number the account should hold

The sixth record is a memo for each brokerage order that should include the following details:

1. Terms and conditions of the order (limit, market, good-til-cancelled, etc.)
2. Any modification or cancellation to the order (either because it was entered incorrectly or the customer changed the order)
3. The account upon which the order was entered
4. The time the order was received
5. The time the order was entered
6. The price at which the order was executed
7. The identity of each person associated with the order
8. The time of execution or cancellation

The seventh record is a memo for each purchase and sale that should include the following details:

1. Price of each security (both per-unit and aggregate price)
2. Time of execution
3. Location of each security (both those in transfer, those awaiting transfer, and those received)
4. Identity of each person associated with the transaction
5. Terms and conditions of the order

The eighth record includes copies of the following:

1. All securities confirmations (both purchases and sales)—the confirmation statement must match up to what was entered for the order and also must match the confirmation statement for the contra party
2. Copies of repurchase and reverse repurchase confirmations—again, these must match the order entry system details and the contra-party paperwork

The ninth record is specifically for cash and margin accounts and must include the following details:

1. The name and address for the owner of each account (if it is a joint account, this is required for each owner)
2. The beneficial owner of each security—this is especially important in a pooled account such as an employee benefit plan
3. The signature of each owner for an account that is margined

The tenth record is for derivative contracts. This record will allow the broker–dealer to determine a variety of information including the inherent risk of the transaction, the calculated value for margin calls, and when options are approaching the end date. The record should include the following details:

1. All puts, calls, spreads, and straddles in which a dealer has a direct or indirect interest
2. All over-the-counter eligible derivative instruments in which the dealer has a direct or indirect interest

The eleventh record is a ledger that must be kept up-to-date at least monthly proving monetary balances so that, when annual reports are filed, there is a monthly report that can be analyzed and used as backup for and ultimately confirmation of final balances. This ledger should include the following:

1. Trial balances
2. Computation of aggregate indebtedness
3. Computation of net capital

The twelfth record is the application for employment for each person associated with the broker–dealer. The application must include the following details:

1. Name, date of birth, address, social security number, and starting date
2. Employment history for the prior 10 years
3. Any details relating to denial, suspension, or revocation of membership or registration or any disciplinary action taken by any federal or state agency or a national securities exchange
4. Any felony arrest record or any securities-related misdemeanor
5. List of any other names by which the employee has been known

The thirteenth record is copies of all X-17F-1A forms filed. Form X-17F-1A is used to report missing, lost, stolen, and counterfeit securities. It is important to keep these forms, especially in the event the securities are eventually recovered. The forms should be kept where they are easily accessible, particularly if there is an ongoing investigation by the Securities & Exchange Commission (SEC) or the Federal Bureau of Investigation (FBI). This record also should include all agreements among reporting institutions regarding registration and all confirmations received from the SEC as a result of inquiry.

Exception to the Rule Requiring a Broker-Dealer to Keep a Record of Employment Details for Each Associated Person

One of the records a broker–dealer is required to keep is a detailed application for employment from each person associated with the firm. The application is required to be accessible and contain employment history for the past 10 years (including an explanation for any gaps in employment during this time period). If the associated person is a registered representative or employment has been approved by a National Securities Exchange (NASDAQ, New York Stock Exchange [NYSE], or American Stock Exchange), then approval will be considered as satisfying this record requirement.

Records That a Broker–Dealer Is Required to Keep for a Period of at Least Six Years

The first 5 records that each broker–dealer is required to keep for a period of 6 years include the following:

1. Blotters, which is a daily record itemizing all sales and purchases, receipts and disbursements of cash, and receipts and deliveries of securities, including names and dates
2. Ledgers that detail all capital accounts, assets, liabilities, and income and expenses
3. Ledgers that detail all pertinent information on a per-customer basis, including debits and credits, sales and purchases, and deliveries of securities, both completed and outstanding
4. Ledgers that detail outstanding security transfers including any that have failed to deliver, dividends and interest received, securities or money loaned or borrowed
5. Ledgers that detail long and short positions for each security including clearance dates and a log of where each security is physically or electronically held

The second set of 5 records that each broker–dealer is required to keep for a period of 6 years includes the following:

1. Memo listing the specific instructions given or received related to the purchase or sale of securities, including changes and cancellations of orders
2. Memo listing purchases and sales including price and time of execution for the account of each member, broker, or dealer

3. Trade confirmations for all purchases and sales
4. Margin records, including the name and address of the owner of any account with an outstanding cash or security margin position
5. Derivative records, including all puts, calls, spreads, and straddles, specifically identifying the units involved

The third set of records that each broker–dealer is required to keep for a period of 6 years includes the following:

1. Trial balance records detailing the aggregate debts and net capital, updated at least once a month
2. A completed employment application for each person associated with a member or broker–dealer, which includes the name (including other names used), address, social security number, date of birth, 10 years of employment history, and information about disciplinary actions
3. Fingerprints for all securities personnel
4. Agreements among reporting institutions and all inquiry confirmations sent from the Securities & Exchange Commission
5. A record of each customer with access to the internal system

The final 6 books or records that each broker–dealer is required to keep for a period of 6 years include:

1. Daily trading summaries, including executed transactions, share volume, and settlement amounts
2. A record related to each account holder, including the name, tax ID number, address, telephone number, date of birth, employment information, annual income, net worth, and investment objectives, including risk tolerance—the customer needs to confirm the information in intervals that do not exceed 36 months
3. Records listing any written complaints received, including confirmation that the customer was given the contact information for the department to which the complaint should be directed
4. A record listing any purchases or sales that are made to someone associated with a member or broker–dealer where the purchase or sale is intended to be compensation
5. A record demonstrating compliance with advertising rules and regulations
6. Contact information for the individuals in each office who can provide details about the types of records kept and how to access them

Records That a Broker–Dealer Is Required to Keep for a Period of Three Years

The first 4 records that a broker–dealer is required to keep for a period of 3 years include the following:

1. All checkbooks, bank statements, cancelled checks, and cash reconciliations
2. Copies of all bills receivable or payable, paid or unpaid, related to the broker–dealer's business
3. Originals of all communications received and copies of all communications sent by the broker–dealer—this includes internal memos relating to the business
4. All trial balances, calculations of aggregate indebtedness, net capital, financial statements, branch office reconciliations, and internal audit papers related to the broker–dealer's business

The second set of 3 records that a broker–dealer is required to keep for a period of 3 years includes the following:

1. All guarantees of accounts and powers of attorney or other evidence provided to grant any discretionary authority over an account and copies of resolutions allowing an agent to act on the behalf of a corporation
2. All written agreements entered into by the broker–dealer related to the business, including agreements related to any accounts
3. All notices related to an internal broker–dealer system provided to the customers of the broker–dealer who sponsors the system

The final book or record that a broker–dealer is required to keep for a period of 3 years is records containing information used to support the annual financial statements including the following:

1. Money balance position (both long and short), including cash and the quantity, price, and valuation of each security in any type of account (secured, partly secured, fully secured, or securities accounts payable) for both customers and noncustomers
2. Amount of secured demand note and a detailed description of collateral securing demand notes, including the name, quantity, and price for each security or cash securing the note
3. Description of futures commodity contracts, including market value and gain or loss position
4. Description of spot commodity positions in customer and noncustomer accounts
5. Description of any put and call options including any that are not in the money
6. Description of all securities in an account that has an outstanding margin balance

Records That a Broker–Dealer Is Required to Keep Related to Those Associated with the Firm

The records that a broker dealer is required to keep related to those associated with the firm include the following:

1. All employment records until 3 years after the termination of the employee
2. All account information until 6 years after the account was closed or transferred
3. Each report requested by a securities regulatory authority for 3 years following the request
4. Each compliance policy or procedures manual created or modified for a period of 3 years following the termination of the policy or manual
5. All reports to review unusual activity in customer accounts for a period of 18 months following the date it was generated

FOCUS Reports That a Broker–Dealer Is Required to File

FOCUS Reports are required whenever a broker–dealer calculates a deduction for the market risk involved in participating in a certain product category. Within 17 business days of the end of each month, the broker–dealer is required to provide the following:

1. A graph reflecting the daily value at risk
2. The aggregate value at risk
3. The market risk deduction taken for each product
4. Credit risk on derivatives exposure, including overall exposure, the amount of the 15 largest potential exposures, the 10 largest commitments, and a summary of current and maximum potential exposures by credit rating

Within 17 business days of the end of each quarter, a broker–dealer is required to file a FOCUS Report detailing the following information:

1. The regular monthly report for the last month in the quarter, which includes a graph reflecting the daily value at risk, the aggregate value at risk, the market risk deduction taken for each product, and credit risk on derivatives exposure, including the following details:
2. Overall exposure
3. The amount of the 15 largest potential exposures
4. The 10 largest commitments
5. Summary of current and maximum potential exposures by credit rating
6. Number of business days that resulted in a net trading loss exceeding the daily value at risk
7. The backtesting results of all internal models used to calculate allowable capital

Audited Customer Statements That a Broker–Dealer Must Be Able to Furnish

Within 105 days after the date the audited financial statements are prepared, a broker–dealer must be able to furnish the following audited information:

1. Balance sheet with auditor's written notes
2. Statement of broker–dealer's actual net capital and its minimum required net capital
3. The most recent Statement of Financial Condition

Customer

In the Securities Exchange Act, the term *customer* is not written in an affirmative way. Instead, it is anyone for whom the broker–dealer holds securities for safekeeping or as collateral who is not one of the following:

1. The broker–dealer
2. A general, special, or limited partner; director; or officer of the broker–dealer
3. A person who contributed part of the capital of the broker–dealer
4. A person who has subordinated claims of the creditors of the broker–dealer

Audited Financial Statements That a Member Must Include in the Annual Filing

A member must include the following audited financial statements in the annual filing with the Securities & Exchange Commission (SEC):

1. A Statement of Financial Condition
2. A Statement of Income
3. A Statement of Cash Flows
4. A Statement of Changes in Stockholders' or Partners'
5. A Statement of Changes in Liabilities
6. Reconciliation of the Computation of Net Capital Computation for Determination of the Reserve Requirements

Procedures That Must Be in Place During the Audit of Financial Statements

When auditing financial statements, there must be procedures in place that are designed to accomplish the following:

1. Identify illegal acts that materially impact the financial statements
2. Identify related party transactions that require additional disclosures
3. Identify the likelihood of whether the company will continue to be in business the following year

Bringing Knowledge of Illegal Acts to the Attention of the Board of Directors

If during the course of an audit, the auditor determines that illegal acts have occurred, the auditor is required to notify the audit committee immediately. If, after making this disclosure, the auditor determines that the audit committee has not sufficiently remedied the situation, then the auditor will bring his or her concerns to the attention of the board of directors. If the board of directors does not take immediate action, then the auditor will provide a copy of the report to the Securities & Exchange Commission.

Minimum Net Capital Rule

Every broker-dealer has a capital amount he or she is required to meet. The minimum amount that must be held depends on the activities that the broker or dealer takes part in. For example, someone who is only a dealer of securities has a lower capital requirement than someone who is a broker. When the net capital falls below the minimum threshold, he or she is required to give notice of the deficiency immediately. In essence, the broker or dealer is indicating that he or she is insolvent.

Sending a Prompt Notification to the Securities & Exchange Commission (SEC)

If, during the course of an audit, the auditor determines that illegal acts have occurred, the auditor is required to notify the audit committee immediately. If, after making this disclosure, the auditor determines that the audit committee has not remedied the situation sufficiently, then the auditor will bring the concerns to the attention of the board of directors. If the board of directors does not take immediate action, then within 48 hours, the auditor must provide a copy of the report to the SEC.

Stolen Security

When a broker-dealer discovers that a security has been stolen (this does not include missing or lost securities, which have their own protocols), he or she should report the theft to the Securities & Exchange Commission (SEC), the Federal Bureau of Investigation (FBI) and the registered transfer agent. At that time, the broker-dealer should be prepared to provide substantiation for the belief that a criminal activity has taken place. The notification must occur within 1 business day of discovering the theft.

Lost or Missing Security

Generally speaking, once it is determined that securities are lost or missing (but no foul play is suspected), the broker-dealer must notify the Securities & Exchange Commission (SEC) and the registered transfer agent within 1 business day. The exception to this rule is if securities are lost or missing while in transit to customers, transfer agents, banks, brokers, dealers, or other reporting institutions. In this situation, the delivering institution must notify the loss to the SEC within a reasonable time period, not to exceed 20 business days from the date of discovery.

Information That Must Be Included When Reporting Lost or Stolen Securities

The following information (if applicable) must be included when a broker–dealer reports lost or stolen securities:

1. Name of issuer
2. Type of security and series
3. Date of issue
4. Maturity date
5. Denomination
6. Interest rate
7. Certificate number
8. Name in which the security is registered
9. Distinguishing characteristics (for counterfeit securities)
10. Date of discovery
11. Committee on Uniform Securities Identification Procedures (CUSIP) number
12. Financial Industry Number Standard (FINS) number
13. Type of loss (missing, lost, or stolen)

Disclosing Financial Condition

A broker–dealer must be willing to disclose his or her financial condition upon request by any customer or regulatory agency. The request may be fulfilled electronically, but the customer must consent to receiving the information in that format by signing a consent form. The statement of financial condition provided must be the most recent version created as either part of the firm's standard practice or the one most recently used to fulfill a regulatory requirement.

Exception to the Rule That Customers Must Receive Account Statements at Least Quarterly

Quarterly account statements are not required if all of the following conditions are met:

1. The account is carried solely on a delivery-versus-payment or receive-versus-payment basis.
2. The account does not show security or money positions at the end of the quarter.
3. The customer consents to suspension of quarterly statements in writing.
4. The broker–dealer provides statements upon request.
5. The broker–dealer agrees to reinstate quarterly statements upon request.

Estimated Value of Direct Participation Program (DPP) and Real Estate Investment Trust (REIT) Securities on Customer Account Statements

In general, Direct Participation Program (DPP) and Real Estate Investment Trust (REIT) securities may be estimated on customer account statements so long as the following conditions are met:

1. The estimated value per share must be the same as what is shown on the annual report.
2. The estimated value is based on data that is no more than 18 months old.
3. A brief description of the estimated value and how it was determined is provided.
4. A disclosure that the assets are generally illiquid is made on the statement.
5. No material change that would seriously impact the pricing of the security has occurred since the last time the valuation of the asset occurred.

Pieces of Information That a Member Must Maintain for Each Account

The 5 pieces of information that a member must maintain for each account include the following:

1. Customer's name and address
2. Whether the customer is of legal age (based on the state of residency)
3. Name of any person associated with or responsible for the account
4. Signature of the partner, officer, or manager indicating that the account has been set up in accordance with all policies and procedures
5. For accounts set up under a legal entity, the name of any person allowed to make trades in the account

Information That Must Be Obtained If the Investments Held Within an Account Are Limited to Open-Ended Shares

If an account is limited to holding only open-ended investment company shares, then prior to the settlement of the first transaction in the account, the member must obtain the following information:

1. The social security number or tax identification number of the customer
2. Occupation of the customer and his or her employer's name and address
3. Whether the customer is associated with any other broker–dealer

Titling of Customer Accounts

When a broker–dealer is titling a customer account, he or she must know the following information:

1. The name and address of the account holder (including any joint account names)
2. Whether the account is for the benefit of another individual (and the name)
3. Whether the account holder is of legal age (and, if not, when he or she becomes the age of majority—this is based on state residency)
4. Whether there are any powers of attorney that need to be considered

Customer Complaints

A customer complaint is defined as any grievance by a customer or any person permitted to act on the behalf of a customer account. Each member must keep a detailed record of all written customer complaints that are related to the office. The report should make clear what actions were taken as a result of the complaint and what response was made to the customer filing the grievance.

Anti-Money Laundering Requirement and Written Policy

Each member firm is required to develop and implement an anti-money laundering compliance program. The program must be developed to ensure that the member is following the requirements of the Bank Secrecy Act and any regulations created by the Department of the Treasury. The plan must be written and signed off on by a member of senior management. The plan must be reviewed with all necessary personnel and revisited on a regular basis to make sure that changes are not necessary.

At a minimum, a member's anti-money laundering policy must include the following:

1. The ability to detect suspicious transactions
2. The causes for reporting suspicious transactions
3. Provisions for annual independent testing by a qualified outside party
4. Contact information for those who are responsible for the daily monitoring of accounts supplied to the Financial Industry Regulatory Authority (FINRA)
5. Provide ongoing training for appropriate personnel.

Ex-Date

With the exception of cash transactions, all securities will be considered ex-dividend, ex-rights, or ex-warrants on a day specifically designated by NASDAQ regulation. This date is based on the value of the distribution, expressed as a percentage of the total value of the security. If this percentage is 25 percent or less, the ex-date will be the record date if the record date falls on a business day. If the record date falls on a nonbusiness day, then the ex-date will be the first business day preceding the record date. If the percentage is greater than 25 percent, then the ex-date will be the first business day after the payable date. In the event that information is not received with enough advance notice to determine the ex-date, NASDAQ will review the facts and circumstances of the distribution to determine the most practical ex-date.

Clearly Erroneous Transactions

A clearly erroneous transaction is one where there is an obvious error in any part of the transaction, including the number of shares (or other unit of trading), the price, or the identification of the security. A transaction that is considered to be clearly erroneous either will be cancelled by both parties involved or will be determined by the Financial Industry Regulatory Authority (FINRA) and subsequently removed from the consolidation tape.

A clearly erroneous transaction can be determined in 2 different ways. The first is if a senior Financial Industry Regulatory Authority (FINRA) official determines that there has been a malfunction in the electronic communication systems requiring that certain transactions be nullified. In the second scenario, when a member receives confirmation that an order was submitted and believes it falls under the clearly erroneous definition, the member has 30 minutes to submit written notice to FINRA's Market Regulation Department. For routed executions to other market centers, members will be permitted an additional 30 minutes to submit a complaint. In certain circumstances known as outlier transactions, FINRA will in its discretion consider complaints submitted after the 30-minute mark but before 60 minutes have passed.

To meet FINRA's definition of an outlier transaction, 1 of the following must be true:

1. The execution price for the security is at least 3 times the numerical guidelines, as referenced under FINRA Rule 11890.
2. The execution price is higher than the 52-week high.
3. The execution price is lower than the 52-week low.

FINRA officials will make a determination as to the validity of the clearly erroneous transaction claim usually within 30 minutes of receipt of the written notice but certainly by opening hour of the next trade day.

For a clearly erroneous transaction on an exchange-listed security to be granted by the Financial Industry Regulatory Authority (FINRA), the price must fall outside the reference price range. The reference price is equal to the consolidated last sale immediately before the execution, with the exception of a multi-stock event involving at least 20 securities.

The following chart provides specific details:

Reference Price, Circumstance, or Product	Regular Trading Hours Numerical Guidelines	Preopening and After-Hours Trading Session Numerical Guidelines
$0.00 < Price ≤ $25.00	10%	20%
$25.00 < Price ≤ $50.00	5%	10%
$50.00 < Price	3%	6%
Multi-Stock Event (involving 5-19 securities, in less than 5 minutes)	10%	10%
Multi-Stock Event (involving more than 20 securities in less than 5 minutes)	30%	30%

Reference Price, Circumstance, or Product	Regular Trading Hours Numerical Guidelines	Preopening and After-Hours Trading Session Numerical Guidelines
Leveraged Exchange-Traded Fund (ETF)/Exchange-Traded Note (ETN) Securities	Regular trading numerical guidelines multiplied by the leverage multiplier (e.g., 2 times)	Regular trading numerical guidelines multiplied by the leverage multiplier (e.g., 2 times)

In the event a member believes that a review of Financial Industry Regulatory Authority's (FINRA's) clearly erroneous transaction decision is warranted, the member may appeal to the Market Operations Review Committee (MORC). The appeal must be made in writing and received within 30 minutes of the original FINRA decision. Once received, the counterparty will be notified of the appeal request, and both parties will have an opportunity to submit any supporting materials that the committee will need to make its decision. The committee will respond with its determination usually the same trading day, but should the appeal request be received after 3:00 pm Eastern Time, the response may not occur until the beginning of the next trading day.

There are no fees for clearly erroneous complaints resulting in a trade being broken up. However, during each calendar month, a member may submit only 2 unsuccessful clearly erroneous complaints without being charged any fees. For any complaints beyond the initial 2, the member will be charged $250 for every unsuccessful complaint during the remainder of the calendar month. These fees are charged on each security involved in the complaint. For example, if a member has already filed 2 unsuccessful complaints, and in the same calendar month, the member files a multi-stock complaint involving 20 securities, and the Financial Industry Regulatory Authority (FINRA) does not find in his or her favor, a separate $250 fee will be assessed for each of the 20 securities involved in the complaint. No fee will be assessed if the member withdraws the complaint prior to FINRA's review. For each appeal to the Market Operations Review Committee, the member will be charged $500 if the committee upholds the original FINRA official's decision. No fee will be assessed should the committee reverse the decision.

For a clearly erroneous transaction to be granted by the Financial Industry Regulatory Authority (FINRA), the price must fall outside the reference price range. The reference price is equal to the consolidated last sale immediately before the execution, with the exception of a multi-stock event involving at least 20 securities. The following chart provides specific details:

Reference Price	Numerical Guidelines (Subject Transaction's % Difference From Reference Price)
$0.9999 and under	20%
$1.00 up to $4.9999	Low end of range minimum 20%
	High end of range minimum 10%

Reference Price	Numerical Guidelines (Subject Transaction's % Difference From Reference Price)
$5.00 up to $74.9999	10%
$75.00 up to $199.9999	Low end of range minimum 10% High end of range minimum 5%
$200.00 up to $499.9999	5%
$500.00 up to $999.9999	Low end of range minimum 5% High end of range minimum 3%
$1,000 and over	3%

Penalties for Violating the Insider Trading & Securities Fraud Enforcement Act of 1988

A person who is found guilty of violating the Insider Trading and Securities Fraud Enforcement Act of 1988 can face a monetary penalty of up to $5 million and imprisonment of up to 20 years. An entity (i.e., not a natural person) faces a penalty of up to $25 million. The statute of limitations under the Insider Trading and Securities Fraud Enforcement Act of 1988 is 5 years from the last day a transaction that violates the act took place.

The person who supervises the violator of the Insider Trading and Securities Act of 1988 may be subject to penalties as well as the actual violator. These penalties include a monetary penalty of the greater of $1 million or 3 times the amount of the profit gained or the amount loss avoided.

Conflict of Interest Involving a Public Offering

In the event that a member has a conflict of interest with a public offering, he or she may participate so long as that member is not primarily responsible nor affiliated with the individual who will be managing the public offering. There must be a prominent disclosure detailing the conflict of interest in the prospectus or offering circular. In addition, a qualified independent underwriter must participate in the preparation of the prospectus and any other registration documents.

A member has a conflict of interest when any of the following circumstances exist:

1. The issuer is controlled by or is under common control with the member, where control equals beneficial ownership of 10 percent or more.
2. Five percent or more of the net offering proceeds will be used to reduce or retire a loan held by the member
3. As a result of the public offering, the member will become an affiliate of the issuer
4. As a result of the public offering, the member will become publicly owned by the issuer
5. As a result of the public offering, the issuer will become a member or form a broker-dealer subsidiary

Time Period Under Which Payment for or Delivery of Securities Must Take Place

In general, a broker–dealer may not enter into a contract in which the payment of funds or delivery of the security takes place later than the third business day after the date of execution. The exceptions to this rule include the following: exempted securities, government securities, municipal securities, commercial paper, bankers' acceptances, commercial bills, contracts involving the purchase or sale of limited partnership interests that are not listed on an exchange, and contracts for the sale of securities that are priced after 4:30 pm Eastern Time and sold on the same day by an issuer to an underwriter. In these situations, the parties involved in the contract will agree on an alternate date for the payment of funds and delivery of the security at the time the contract is entered into.

Delivery Requirements That Must Be Met in the Settlement of Contracts

In general, NASDAQ regulations will dictate the delivery requirements of contracts, including the date of delivery. These same rules direct that the delivery must take place at the office of the purchaser on the same day that funds are paid. If NASDAQ regulations are silent as to the delivery date for a specific type of contract, the delivery may take place on the business day following the one in which the seller provides written notice of intent to deliver. Even in these instances though, the delivery will take place at the office of the purchaser.

Scenarios Under Which Contracts May Be Cancelled

According to NASDAQ regulations, a contract may be cancelled under the following conditions:

1. In order to rectify conflicts involving the settlement of the contract
2. If the underlying securities are not going to be issued or distributed
3. If the underlying securities materially change prior to distribution—this includes changes in the redemption schedule, dividend payments, interest rates, maturity, yield, and exercise price
4. If there are certain other changes, including changes in the value of the securities, restructuring of the financial arrangements previously indicated by the issuer, and settlement of a previously outstanding legal action that has resulted in significant material change of the issuer

Continuing Education Requirements for Those Who Are Registered

Continuing education is required for certain registered people after they have passed their initial qualifying examinations. The purpose of the continuing education is to make certain that the member is kept up-to-date with changes to rules and quiz the member on ethical standards. The continuing education requirements consist of a regulatory element and a firm element. The regulatory element is performed by the Financial Industry Regulatory Authority (FINRA). Once a member has held his or her registration for a period of 2 years, they must participate in regulatory training. From that point on, it is required every 3 years. The individual has 120 days to complete the training (from the due date) or else the registration will be made inactive until the training is completed. The firm element is a continuing education program administered by the member firm. It is required to be delivered to all locations where people are registered and must touch on the topics of general investment features and their associated risk factors, suitability and sales practice considerations, applicable regulatory requirements, and training on ethics.

Becoming a Financial Industry Regulatory Authority (FINRA) Member

Any registered broker, dealer, municipal securities broker or dealer, or government securities broker–dealer authorized to transact and whose regular course of business consists in actually transacting and any branch of the investment banking or securities business in United States are eligible for membership in a corporation (i.e., Financial Industry Regulatory Authority [FINRA]) except those who are not eligible to join FINRA, including those who do not comply with bylaws and regulations, do not pass background checks, or are subsequently suspended or expelled from FINRA.

Those wishing to become members of Financial Industry Regulatory Authority (FINRA) should apply through the electronic process and complete the forms, including an agreement to comply with federal securities laws, the rules and regulations of FINRA, National Association of Securities Dealers (NASD) regulation, and NAS dispute resolution. They also must complete an agreement promising to pay dues, assessments, and other charges and sanctions imposed by the corporation. Applicants also promise to supply reasonable information as the corporation may require to verify identity and confirm that the member is in good standing with all rules and regulations. In general, FINRA members may not transfer their membership to others. However in the event of a consolidation, reorganization, merger, change of name or similar change at a corporate level, an exception is available to allow FINRA members to transfer their memberships without going through the application process again. In addition, the death, change of name, withdrawal of any partner, addition of a new partner, or change in legal structure will not require a new application by FINRA members employed by that firm.

Executive Representative

Each member will appoint and certify to the secretary of the corporation 1 executive representative. This person will represent, vote, and act for the member in all affairs of the corporation except that other executives of the member also may hold office in the corporation, serve on the board or committees, or otherwise take part in the affairs of the corporation. A member may change its executive representative by giving notice via electronic process or by meeting other protocols required by the corporation.

Ways in Which a FINRA Application May Be Delivered

For purposes of the Financial Industry Regulatory Authority (FINRA), an application may be delivered in the following ways and be deemed completed:

1. Via United States Postal Service (USPS) by requesting first-class mail delivery.
2. Via overnight courier as specified by the airbill
3. Via service or filing by hand delivery (keep the receipt as evidence of delivery)
4. Via service or filing by fax (keep the written confirmation page as evidence of delivery)
5. Filing via electronic system (based on the confirmation date)

Items That Must Be Included in an Application for FINRA Membership

1. Form NMA
2. An original signed and notarized Form BD with applicable schedules
3. An original Financial Industry Regulatory Authority (FINRA)-approved fingerprint card for each associated person
4. A new member assessment report
5. A detailed business plan that adequately describes al material aspects of the business that will be performed at and after the initiation of business operations
6. A monthly projection of income and expenses
7. An organizational chart
8. The intended location of the applicant's principal place of business and all other offices
9. A description of the method and media to be employed to develop a customer base
10. A description of the business facilities including the final lease
11. The number of markets to be made
12. Any plan to enter into contractual commitments such as underwritings
13. Any plan to distribute or maintain securities in proprietary products
14. A description of communications and operational systems the applicant will employ to conduct business with customers
15. A copy of any decision by a federal or state authority
16. A list of all associated persons
17. Documentation of the following events:
18. Regulatory action against or investigation of the applicant or associated person
19. Investment-related civil action
20. Investment-related complaint
21. Criminal action filed against the applicant or associated person (not traffic related)
22. Copy of any document that provides evidence of termination for cause
23. Description of any remedial action required

24. Copy of final or proposed contracts with banks, clearing entities, or service bureaus
25. Financial controls to be put in place
26. Supervisory controls to be put in place
27. Description of the experience of supervisors and principals
28. Proposed record keeping system
29. Copy of the firm's written training plan to comply with the firm's element of continuing education requirements

PRINCIPAL

A principal is someone who is engaged actively in the management of a firm's investment banking or securities business, including supervision, solicitation, conduct of business, or the training of people associated with 1 of these functions. To become a principal, an application must be submitted to Financial Industry Regulatory Authority (FINRA) and a qualifying test must be successfully passed. With the exception of a sole proprietor, each National Association of Securities Dealers (NASD) member firm must have at least 2 officers or partners who are registered as principals. Examples of a principal include the following:

1. Sole proprietors
2. Officers
3. Partners
4. Managers of offices of supervisory jurisdiction
5. Directors of corporations

Besides General Principal, which is the required classification for the chief compliance officer of a firm, there are a variety of other principal titles that a person may hold, including these:

- Limited Principal—Investment Company and Variable Contracts: This is someone who will have supervisory responsibility over the conduct of business in an investment company and variable contract products only.
- Limited Principal—Financial and Operations: The chief financial officer generally has this title; however, anyone who has the responsibility of preparing or approving the accuracy of financial reports can hold this title.
- Limited Principal—Registered Options and Securities Features: Every person engaged in the supervision of options and security futures sales practices should be registered under this classification.
- Limited Principal—General Securities Sales Supervisor: Anyone with supervisory responsibilities that are limited to investment banking and securities should be registered under this classification.
- Limited Principal—Municipal Securities: Anyone who is engaged in the management or supervision of only the member's municipal securities business can be registered under this classification.

- Limited Principal—Government Securities: Anyone who is engaged in the management or supervision of only the member's US government securities business can be registered under this classification.

Representative

A representative is a person associated with a member (other than a principal) who is engaged in the investment banking or securities business for the member, including the functions of supervision, solicitation, or conduct business in securities. This category also includes those who train those who perform any of these actions. Most people will receive the classification of general securities representative; however, if the job functions are limited to certain securities or business functions, they can apply to be limited representatives. The available limited classifications include the following:

1. Limited Representative—Investment Company and Variable Contracts Products
2. Limited Representative—Direct Participation Programs
3. Limited Representative—Options and Securities Futures
4. Limited Representative—Corporate Securities
5. Limited Representative—Equity Trader
6. Limited Representative—Government Securities
7. Limited Representative—Private Securities Offerings
8. Limited Representative—Investment Banking

Assistant Representatives

Anyone who works for a member firm and who is hired to perform the duties of an assistant representative is required to register with Financial Industry Regulatory Authority (FINRA). An assistant representative is someone who accepts unsolicited customer orders and submits them for execution. Because part of the job includes order processing, they are required to register. These individuals are required to pass a qualifying examination. For someone who previously passed the test and then for a period of 2 years does not perform these job functions (i.e., they leave the firm or accept another position within the same firm), it will be necessary to retake the qualifying exam.

Registration Exemptions

There are certain circumstances under which someone is exempt from registration. These include the following:

1. Those whose functions are solely clerical
2. Those who are not actively engaged in the investment banking or securities business
3. Those whose functions are related exclusively to the member firm's need for nominal corporate officers or for capital participation

4. Those associated with a member whose functions relate solely to transactions on the floor of a national securities exchange (who they are registered with), transactions in municipal securities, transactions in commodities, and transactions in security futures (assuming that the person is registered with a registered futures association)

Qualification Examinations

Qualification examinations are tests that members take in order to perform certain job functions with their firms. The examinations contain a series of questions that are limited to the specific rules and regulations that are required to be known to perform the new job function. The exams are created by the board of governors who release a study outline to allow the test taker to have the opportunity to study what will be covered on the specific examination. In certain cases, the National Association of Securities Dealers (NASD) may waive the requirement to take the examination and accept other standards as evidence of the applicant's qualifications. Advanced age or physical infirmity alone will not be enough to constitute waiving the exam. Experience in fields similar to investment banking or securities business may constitute sufficient grounds for the waiver to be granted; however, it truly is on a case-by-case scenario. If the individual fails to pass the qualifying exam, he or she may take it again after a period of 30 days has passed; anyone who fails 3 or more times in succession may not take the test again until a period of 180 days has passed.

Proxy and Other Issuer-Related Materials That a Member Is Required to Process and Forward to the Finra for Equity and Debt Securities

For equity securities, the member is required to process and forward all proxy material and annual reports that were sent to stockholders. For debt securities, the member is required to process and forward all documents prepared by or on behalf of the issuer or the trustee on a specific issue of the security, notices concerning monetary or technical defaults, financial reports, information statements, and material event notices. For purposes of proxy materials, the issuer must ensure that there are sufficient copies of the materials so that each registered holder of a member has an opportunity to receive it. In addition, the issuer must provide assurance that he or she will reimburse the member for all out-of-pocket costs incurred with the solicitation, including reasonable clerical expenses.

Creating Networking Arrangements Between Members and Financial Institutions

The following considerations must be made when networking arrangements between members and financial institutions are being created:

1. Setting: If a member provides brokerage services on the premises of a financial institution, there must be Also addition, the member's name must be clearly visible and kept as separate as possible from the routine deposit-taking activities of the financial institution.

2. Networking Arrangement: There must be a clearly written compensation arrangement that complies with all broker–dealer obligations and stipulates that the Securities & Exchange Commission (SEC) and the Financial Industry Regulatory Authority (FINRA) will be allowed to access the premises to inspect books and records kept by the broker–dealer.
3. Customer Disclosure: Prior to the time that a customer account is opened, the member must disclose in writing that the services are being provided by the member and not by the financial institution and that any securities purchased are not protected by the Financial Industry Regulatory Authority (FDIC) and are subject to investment risk.
4. Communications With the Public: Any marketing materials that mention the location of the broker–dealer must indicate specifically that brokerage services are being provided by the member firm and not the financial institution.

Trading with Nonmembers

A nonmember broker or dealer is anyone who uses mail as his or her main means of gaining sales of securities and is not a member of any securities association, except those who exclusively deal in commercial paper, bankers' acceptances, and commercial bills. The following restrictions exist when transacting with nonmembers:

1. No selling concessions, discounts or other allowances are allowed to a member of the public.
2. Joining with any nonmember broker or dealer in a syndicate group to sell a security is not permitted.
3. Selling a security to or buying a security from a nonmember broker or dealer at the same price at which the member would buy or sell the security to a person who is a member is not permitted.

Situations Under Which an Offering Is Considered Exempt from SEC Registration

The following are considered exempt from Securities & Exchange (SEC) registration:

1. Securities offered by corporate, foreign government, or foreign government agency that have unsecured nonconvertible debt with a term of at least 4 years or nonconvertible preferred debt rated by a nationally recognized statistical rating organization with 1 of its 4 highest ratings.
2. Nonconvertible debt securities and nonconvertible preferred debt rated by a nationally recognized statistical rating organization with 1 of its 4 highest ratings.
3. Securities registered with the Securities & Exchange Commission (SEC) on Form S-3 or F-3
4. Foreign private issuer incorporated under the laws of Canada
5. Securities pursuant to a firm commitment underwriting arrangement
6. Financing instrument-backed securities rated by a nationally recognized statistical rating organization with 1 of its 4 highest ratings.

7. Exchange offers where the securities will be issued on the NASDAQ or New York Stock Exchange (NYSE)
8. Offerings of securities by a church or charitable institution
9. Offerings of securities by a pooled investment vehicle
10. Any exchange offer, merger, or acquisition that results in direct or indirect public ownership of the member

Private Placement

A private placement is a sale of securities to a relatively small number of select investors as a means of raising capital. These types of sales are nonpublic offerings and are subject to an exemption under the Securities Act. Investors involved in private placements are often banks, mutual funds, insurance companies, and pension funds. In general, 85 percent of the proceeds must be used for a state business purpose. The disclosure requirements that accompany a private placement include the following:

1. If there is a private placement memorandum or term sheet addressing the intended use of the proceeds and the expenses and selling compensation will be paid to the member, it must be provided
2. If there is not a private placement memorandum or term sheet, then the member must prepare an offering document that addresses the use of the proceeds and the expenses and selling compensation that will be paid to the member.

Exemptions to the Rule That at Least 85 Percent of the Offering Proceeds in a Private Placement Must Be Used for Business Purposes

The exemptions to the rule that at least 85 percent of the offering proceeds from a private placement be used for a stated business purpose include those sold exclusively to the following:

1. Institutional accounts
2. Qualified purchasers, defined as a natural person who owns at least $5 million in liquid investments (i.e., does not include illiquid or tangible personal property)
3. Qualified institutional buyers, that is, entities including banks, savings and loans associations, insurance companies, investment companies, and employee benefit plans as referenced in Rule 144A
4. Investment companies formed under the Investment Company Act
5. An entity made up exclusively of qualified institutional buyers
6. Banks as defined by Section 3 of the Securities Act

The other exemptions to the rule that at least 85 percent of the offering proceeds from a private placement be used for a stated business purpose include the following:

1. Offerings of exempted securities (as referenced in the Securities Act)
2. Offerings made under Rule 144A or Regulation S

3. Offerings where the member acts in a wholesaling capacity
4. Offerings with short-term maturities as referenced in the Securities Act
5. Offerings of subordinated loans under Securities Exchange act (SEA) Rule 15c3-1
6. Offerings of variable contracts
7. Offerings of guaranteed annuity contracts
8. Offerings of unregistered investment-grade debt and preferred securities
9. Offerings to employees of the issuer
10. Offerings of a commodity pool
11. Offerings of equity and credit derivatives

Supervisory System That a Firm Must Put in Place

The Financial Industry Regulatory Authority (FINRA) requires that a firm put in place a supervisory system, and it needs to take into consideration the following:

1. The system should supervise effectively the activities of each registered representative, registered principal, and those associated with them.
2. The system should ensure that the company is in compliance with applicable National Association of Securities Dealers (NASD) rules.
3. The supervisory system should include written policies and procedures.
4. The designation of the registered principal who will have final authority to oversee the procedures should be identified.
5. The written plan should identify which offices will be considered offices of supervisory jurisdiction. Not all offices have to be given this title—to an extent, it is based on how many offices are in a geographic area and whether they act independently of one another.
6. Reasonable efforts to train anyone who will be supervising others should be made.

Written Procedures That a Firm Must Have in Place

The Financial Industry Regulatory Authority (FINRA) requires that firms put in place written procedures designed to supervise the activities of registered personnel (representatives and principals). The procedures should take into consideration the following:

1. Tape Recording of Conversations: The taping of all telemarketing activities for registered persons is required to be kept for at least 3 years, and by the 30th day of the month following the end of each quarter, each firm should submit to National Association of Securities Dealers (NASD) a report on the supervision of the telemarketing activities of its registered personnel.
2. Internal Inspections: At least once per year, each member should look at his or her policies and procedures to ensure that violations of NASD rules are not occurring and review any irregularities and abuses. Offices that are not considered offices of supervisory jurisdiction may be reviewed once every 3 years.

3. Review of Transactions and Correspondence: Each member should review the transactions and incoming and outgoing correspondence for each of its registered representatives, with an eye on providing additional training where needed
4. Qualifications Investigated: Each member should ensure that personnel represent the firm with good character, appropriate background, and experience and business reputation.
5. Outside Business Activities: Each member should have a plan for members to request association with an outside business activity

Permissible and Restricted Private Securities Transactions

Prior to participating in any private securities transaction, an associated person must give written notice to the member detailing the proposed transaction and state whether he or she may receive selling compensation with the transaction. In the case where the transaction will result in selling compensation, the member must indicate approval or rejection of the proposed transaction prior to purchase. If the member does not approve of the transaction, the associated person is not allowed to take part in it. In the event where the transaction will not result in selling compensation, only an acknowledgement is required from the member. However, he or she may choose to request that the person adhere to specified conditions in connection with his or her participation in the transaction.

Business Continuity Plan

A member firm's business continuity plan is written to address emergencies that could lead to significant business disruptions. By having a plan in place, brokers can continue to provide services to their customers. Each member must conduct an annual review of its business continuity plan to determine if any modifications are necessary. The plan should take the following items (at a minimum) into consideration:

1. Data backup and recovery
2. All mission-critical systems
3. Financial and operational assessments
4. Alternate communications between customers and the member
5. Alternate communications between the member and its employees
6. Alternate physical location for employees to report
7. Critical business constituent, bank, and counterparty impact
8. Regulatory reporting
9. Communications with regulators
10. How the member will assure customers that they still have prompt access to their funds

Prohibited Activities Specifically Referenced by the New York Stock Exchange (NYSE) That May Lead to Suspension or Termination of Membership

The following activities may lead to suspension or termination of membership:

1. Violation of the Securities Exchange Act
2. Violation of agreements with the exchange
3. Violation of rules adopted by the exchange board of directors
4. Making a material misstatement to the exchange
5. Effecting any transaction in or inducing the purchase or sale by manipulative, deceptive, or other fraudulent device
6. Failing to observe high standards of commercial honor
7. Acts detrimental to the interest or welfare of the exchange
8. Refusing or failing to comply with a request of the exchange to submit books and records

Sanctions That the FINRA May Enforce Due to Violation of 1 or More of Its Rules

The Financial Industry Regulatory Authority (FINRA) may impose 1 or more of the following sanctions on a member who violates 1 or more of its rules:

1. Censure a member
2. Impose a fine
3. Suspend membership
4. Revoke membership
5. Suspend a person from association with all members
6. Impose a temporary or permanent cease-and-desist order
7. Impose any other fitting sanction

FINRA Arbitration Process

The order of the arbitration process is as follows:

1. A claim is filed that details the facts and the requested remedy.
2. The respondent files a statement answering the claim detailing all necessary facts and available defenses to the claim.
3. An arbitrator panel is selected to hear the case.
4. The arbitrator panel meets with the parties involved to schedule hearing dates and go through any preliminary issues.
5. There is a period of discovery in which an exchange of documents and information about the claim takes place.
6. There are hearings in which the parties and arbitrators meet to present arguments and evidence in support of their positions.
7. The arbitrators take time to deliberate the facts and ultimately render a written decision.

UNIFORM PRACTICE CODE

The Uniform Practice Code (UPC) is a set of standards that governs all over-the-counter (OTC) secondary market transactions between members. This includes the rights and liabilities of members participating in a transaction. All transactions are subject to the UPC except the following:

1. Transactions in securities between members which are compared, cleared, or settled through the facilities of a registered clearing agency
2. Transactions in securities exempted under Section 3 of the Exchange Act
3. Transactions in municipal securities under Section 3 of the Exchange Act
4. Transactions in redeemable securities issued by a company registered under the Investment Company Act

PROVISIONS THAT WILL APPLY TO TRANSACTIONS THAT TRADE FLAT

All transactions in bonds that are traded flat will be ex-interest at the following times:

1. On the record date if the record date falls on a business day
2. On the first business day preceding the record date if the record date falls on a day other than a business day
3. On the first business day preceding the date on which an interest payment is to be made if no record day is fixed
4. If notice of payment of interest is not released early enough, the security will be ex-interest on the first business day as is practical

BOOK-ENTRY SETTLEMENT RULES

The book-entry settlement rules in Uniform Practice Code (UPC) Rule 11310 dictate the following:

1. A member must use the facilities of a securities depository for the book-entry settlement of all transactions in depository-eligible securities with another member of a national exchange.
2. A member cannot trade delivery-versus-payment or receipt-versus-payment transactions in a depository-eligible security with a customer unless the transaction is settled by book entry using the facilities of a securities depository.
3. This rule is not for transactions outside the United States or those that are for same-day settlement if the deliverer is unable to deposit the securities prior to the cutoff.

Buy-in Procedures and Requirements

A securities contract that has not been completed by the seller according to its terms may be closed by the buyer no sooner than the third business day following the date delivery was due. This rule does not apply to the following:

1. Where the contract is subject to buy-in requirements of a national securities exchange or a registered clearing agency
2. Transactions in securities exempted under Section 3 of the Exchange Act
3. Transactions in municipal securities under section 3 of the Exchange Act
4. Transactions in redeemable securities issued by companies registered by the Investment Company Act
5. Transactions in direct participation program securities

Buy-in Notice

Written notice of buy-in must be delivered to the seller at his or her office no later than 12 noon, 2 business days preceding the execution of the proposed buy-in. The definition of written notice includes an electronic notice through a medium that provides for an immediate return receipt capability. Confirmation of receipt notice by the seller should be maintained as part of the buyer's books and records. If the seller does not accept the buy-in, a written response should be sent no later than 6:00 on the date of the issuance of the buy-in notice. A re-transmittal of the notice of buy-in should be delivered no later than 12 noon the following day if no response is received from the counteragent.

Sellout

In the event that a buyer fails to accept the terms of delivery in a contract, and lacking a properly executed Uniform Reclamation Form or equivalent, the seller may sell out in the best available market. To do so, the party executing the sellout needs to notify the broker–dealer for whose account and risk such securities were sold of the quantity of securities sold and the price received. The notification needs to be in writing. The definition of written notice includes an electronic notice through a medium that provides for an immediate return receipt capability. A formal confirmation of the sale must be forwarded as promptly as possible after the execution of the sellout.

Rights and Warrants

Rights are a privilege offered to holders of a security to purchase new shares issued by the corporation at a predetermined price, which is normally discounted to the market price. The number of shares the holder is able to purchase is in direct proportion to the number of shares initially owned. Rights are also known as subscription rights. A warrant is a derivative security that gives the holder the right to purchase a security (usually an equity) from the issuer at a specific price at a certain time. Warrants often are included in a new debt issue to entice investors to purchase it. For both rights and warrants, the unit of trading is 100.

Cash-on-Delivery (COD) Orders

Members are not permitted to accept an order from a customer including foreign customers or broker-dealers unless all of the following procedures are followed:

1. The member received the order from a known customer.
2. There is a note on file that it is a payment-on-delivery or collect-on-delivery transaction.
3. The member delivers the confirmation no later than the close of business the day after execution.
4. The member obtained an agreement that the customer will provide its agent the delivery or receipt instructions.

Assignment and Power of Substitution Requirements

For a registered security to be considered a good delivery, it must be accompanied by an assignment and power of substitution. An assignment can be executed on the certificate itself or on a separate paper. The signature to an assignment or power of substitution must be technically correct—there cannot be any alternation or enlargement other than *and* can be written "&" and *Company* can be written "Co." A certificate registered in the names of 2 or more individuals or firms must be signed by all owners. Any correction to an assignment or power of substitution must be accompanied by an explanation signed by the person or firm.

Glossary

Bonds

For bonds, the underlying unit of delivery is $1,000 for bearer bonds, and for registered bonds, it is multiples of $1,000 up to $100,000.

Controlling

Controlling means the power to direct or cause the direction of management and policies of a person, whether through ownership of voting stock, direction of the management, or development of policies and procedures. A person who is the owner of more than 20 percent or more of voting stock automatically is considered a controlling interest, as are members of the board of directors and certain other key employees.

Default Upon Redemption of Due Bills

Default upon redemption of due bills is a term that is used when the due bill on a security is not honored by the seller.

Delegation Plan

A delegation plan is a plan of allocation and delegation of functions by the National Association of Securities Dealers (NASD) to subsidiaries as approved by the Securities & Exchange Commission (SEC).

Due Bills

The term due bill is an instrument used to provide evidence of a transfer of title to any security or rights of a seller to a subsequent purchaser.

Due Bill Checks

The term due bill check is used to mean that a check is payable on the date of payment of a cash dividend, interest on registered bonds, or interest on unit investment trust

Due Bills for Stock Dividends and Rights

Due bill for stock dividends and rights is used when a security is sold before it trades ex-dividends or ex-rights and delivered too late to transfer on or before the record date.

Irregular Delivery

Irregular delivery includes wrong, duplicate, misdirected or over-deliveries. In the event of an irregular delivery, reclamation should be made within 30 months.

Large Firm

Large firm means any broker or dealer admitted to membership in the corporation that, at the time of determination, has at least 500 or more registered representatives.

Lost, Stolen, or Confiscated Securities

Securities that were previously reported as lost, stolen, or confiscated will be rejected, and reclamation should be made within 30 months.

Midsize Firm

Midsize firm means any broker or dealer admitted to membership in the corporation that, at the time of determination, has between 100 and 499 registered representatives.

Running of 30 Month Period

Running of 30-month period refers to the amount of time that exists for the reclamation process to be initiated. The period begins on the settlement date.

Small Firm

Small firm means any broker or dealer admitted to membership in the corporation that, at the time of determination, has less than 100 registered representatives.

Stocks

For stocks, the underlying unit of delivery is 100 shares. Shares that are not a multiple of 100 are considered odd lots.

Transfer Refused

Transfer refused is when a specific certificate tendered has been refused by the transfer agent. It should be returned within 30 months after the settlement date.

Unit Investment Trust Securities

For unit investment trust securities, the minimum unit of delivery is a single unit of the trust.

Net Capital Requirements

Financial Scenarios Under Which a Member Firm Must Provide Written Notification to the FINRA

The first 3 financial scenarios under which a member firm must provide written notification to the Financial Industry Regulatory Authority (FINRA) are these:

1. If its net capital falls below 150 percent of its minimum dollar net capital requirement
2. If the member is subject to the aggregate indebtedness requirement and the amount is more than 1,000 percent of its net capital
3. If the member elects to use the alternative method of computing net capital, and the amount is less than 1 of the specified dollar amounts in the Securities Exchange Act.

The last 3 financial scenarios under which a member firm must provide written notification to the Financial Industry Regulatory Authority (FINRA) are these:

1. The member elects to use the alternative method for computing net capital, and the tentative net capital is less than 50 percent of the early warning notification or less than $1.25 billion.
2. The member is registered as a futures commission merchant, and its net capital is less than 120 percent of the minimum risk-based capital requirements of the Commodity Exchange Act.
3. The member's deduction of capital withdrawals during the next 6 months would result in breaking any net capital requirement rule.

Aggregate Indebtedness Standard

The aggregate indebtedness standard states that broker-dealers are not allowed to permit its aggregate indebtedness to exceed 1500 percent of its net capital or 800 percent of its net capital for 12 months after establishing the business. There is an alternative standard that broker-dealers are permitted to elect rather than use this standard.

Minimum Capital Requirements

A broker-dealer who carries customer accounts and receives or holds funds in these accounts must hold a minimum of $250,000 in net capital. A broker-dealer will be considered to be holding securities for its customers unless delivery of securities to another firm occurs promptly.

A municipal securities broker is someone who exclusively acts as an agent in the purchase or sale of municipal securities, has no customers, and does not maintain proprietary accounts. For those meeting this definition, the minimum net capital that must be maintained is $150,000.

A dealer is required to hold at least $100,000 of net capital. A dealer includes anyone who endorses or writes options other than those on a registered national securities exchange and has more than 10 transactions in any 1 calendar year for its own investment account. It does not apply to people engaging only in underwriting activities.

A broker–dealer who introduces customer accounts and receives securities must maintain at least $50,000 of net capital. This category includes anyone who introduces transactions and accounts of customers to another registered broker–dealer who carries the accounts on a fully disclosed basis and receives but does not hold securities. This category includes those who are participating in a firm commitment underwriting but who do not enter into a commitment for the purchase of the shares.

A broker–dealer engaged in the sale of redeemable shares of registered investment companies is required to maintain a net capital of at least $25,000. This category includes those who act as a broker or dealer in the purchase, sale, and redemption of redeemable shares of registered investment companies but promptly transmit or deliver all funds or shares.

A broker–dealer who does not carry accounts for customers and does not engage in the act of receiving or holding funds for customers must meet a minimum capital requirement of $5,000. A dealer who acts in a principal capacity only falls under this category, so long as any shares are cleared through another registered member.

A broker–dealer who engages in market making must maintain a net capital of at least $2,500 for each security, unless the market value is less than $5, in which case the minimum net capital is $1,000 per security. The maximum net capital amount for market makers is $1,000,000. The Securities & Exchange Commission (SEC) may allow the market maker to use the market risk standards for over-the-counter (OTC) derivatives; however, an OTC derivatives dealer must maintain a tentative net capital of at least $100 million and net capital of at least $20 million.

A broker–dealer engaging in reverse repurchase agreements must maintain net capital equal to 10 percent of the following:

1. The excess of the market value of Treasury bills, bonds, and notes subject to reverse repurchase agreements with any 1 party over 105 percent of the contract prices
2. The excess of the market value of securities guaranteed as to principal or interest by a US agency with any 1 party over 110 percent of the contract prices
3. The excess of the market value of securities subject to reverse repurchase agreements with any 1 party over 120 percent of the contract prices

ALTERNATIVE NET CAPITAL COMPUTATION FOR BROKER–DEALERS WHO CHOOSE TO BE SUPERVISED ON A CONSOLIDATED BASIS

A broker–dealer may complete an application with the Securities & Exchange Commission (SEC) to request that he or she be allowed to calculate net capital using the market risk standards to compute a deduction for market risk. They also may apply to use the credit risk standards to compute a deduction for credit risk. To be eligible, the broker–dealer must maintain a tentative net capital of at least $1 billion and net capital of at least $500 million.

EXCLUSIONS FROM THE AGGREGATE INDEBTEDNESS STANDARD

The first 5 exclusions from the aggregate indebtedness standard are these:

1. Indebtedness that is collateralized by securities that are carried long by the broker
2. Amounts payable against securities loaned if carried long by the broker
3. Amounts payable against securities failed to receive that are carried long by the broker
4. Credit balances in accounts representing amounts payable for securities or money market instruments not yet received but are not outstanding for more than 3 business days
5. Equities held in accounts segregated according to the Commodity Exchange Act

The second set of 5 exclusions from the aggregate indebtedness standard are these:

1. Liability reserves maintained for refunds of charges but only to the extent of amounts on deposit
2. Amounts payable for qualified securities deposited into a "Special Reserve Bank Account for the Exclusive Benefit of Customers"
3. Fixed liabilities that are secured by assets used as part of the ordinary course of business
4. Open contractual commitment liabilities
5. Indebtedness subordinated to the claims of creditors

The last set of 5 exclusions from the aggregate indebtedness standard are these:

1. Liabilities effectively subordinated to the claims of creditors
2. Credit balances in accounts of general partners
3. Deferred tax liabilities
4. 85 percent of amounts payable to a registered investment company related to fail-to-deliver receivables
5. 85 percent of the amounts payable against securities loaned for which the broker has receivables borrowed

Adjustments to Unrealized Profit and Loss and Deferred Taxes on a Net Worth Statement

The first 3 adjustments to profit and loss and deferred taxes are these:

1. All long and short securities and commodities are marked to market value.
2. For call options, if the market value of the underlying security is less than the exercise price, it will have no value.
3. For put options, if the market value of the underlying security is more than the exercise price, it will have no value.

The second set of 3 adjustments to profit and loss and deferred taxes are these:

1. Add to the net worth the deferred income tax liability (federal and state).
2. Deduct any deferred tax liability related to accrued income.
3. Deduct any deferred tax liability related to the unrealized appreciation in assets.

The last 3 adjustments to profit and loss and deferred taxes are these:

1. Add the future income tax benefits arising from unrealized losses.
2. Add actual liability related to accrued income.
3. Add unrealized profits and deduct unrealized losses in the account of the broker–dealer.

Rules That Sole Proprietors May Follow Related to the Net Worth Statement

If a broker–dealer is employed as a sole proprietor (i.e., not formed as a partnership or a corporation), he or she may be permitted to exclude a portion of the liability if it was not 100 percent incurred for business use. The specific amount of the exclusion will be equal to the difference between the total liability and the amount that was used during in the course of business.

Rules Related the Deduction of Assets That Are Not Readily Convertible to Cash

Members are permitted to deduct fixed assets and those that are not readily convertible to cash. This includes the following items:

1. Real estate
2. Furniture and fixtures
3. Exchange memberships
4. Prepaid rent

REPORTING DIFFERENCES BASED UPON PERCENTAGE OF MARKET VALUE

The number of business days that a member has to report differences depends on the market value of the security. The following chart depicts the information.

Percentage of Market Value	Number of Business Days
25%	7 days
50%	14 days
75%	21 days
100%	28 days

SECURITIES HAIRCUT

A securities haircut is the percentage that may be subtracted from the market value of a security that is being used as collateral. The percentage that can be subtracted is based on the underlying asset. The following chart demonstrates the permissible haircut for securities that have a guaranteed principal or interest provision.

Time Until Maturity	Haircut Percentage
0–3 months	0%
3–6 months	0.5%
6–9 months	0.75%
9–12 months	1%
1–2 years	1.5%
2–3 years	2%
3–5 years	3%
5–10 years	4%
10–15 years	4.5%
15–20 years	5%
20–25 years	5.5%
More than 25 years	6%

The following chart demonstrates the permissible haircut for municipal securities that do not have a guaranteed interest or principal provision and have a duration of 731 days or less.

Time Until Maturity	Haircut Percentage
Less than 30 days	0%
30–91 days	0.125%
91–181 days	0.25%
181–271 days	0.375%
271–366 days	0.5%
366–456 days	0.75%
456–731 days	1%

The following chart demonstrates the permissible haircut for municipal securities that do not have a guaranteed interest or principal provision and have a duration of greater than 2 years.

Time Until Maturity	Haircut Percentage
Less than 1 year	1%
1- 2 years	2%
2-3.5 years	3%
3.5-5 years	4%
5-7 years	5%
7-10 years	5.5%
10-15 years	6%
15-20 years	6.5%
Greater than 20 years	7%

The following chart demonstrates the permissible haircut for commercial paper, bankers' acceptances, and certificates of deposit (CDs).

Time Until Maturity	Haircut Percentage
Less than 30 days	0%
30-91 days	0.125%
91-181 days	0.25%
181-271 days	0.375%
271 days-1 year	0.5%
Greater than 1 year	0.75%

The following chart demonstrates the permissible haircut for nonconvertible debt securities.

Time Until Maturity	Haircut Percentage
Less than 1 year	2%
1-2 years	3%
2-3 years	5%
3-5 years	6%
5-10 years	7%
10-15 years	7.5%
15-20 years	8%
20-25 years	8.5%
Greater than 25 years	9%

MARKET MAKER

A market maker is any specialist who is permitted to act as a dealer in the capacity of a block positioner and enters quotations in the inter-dealer system as willing to buy or sell for his or her own account on a regular or continual basis. To become a NASDAQ market maker, one must enter a registration request via a NASDAQ electronic interface or contact NASDAQ market operations. The registration becomes effective on the same day the request is entered into the system. Only a registered market maker can enter a quotation or a quotation size. Failure to enter a quotation within 5 business days after registration in a security will result in termination of registration.

SITUATIONS IN WHICH A BROKER–DEALER MAY MARK AN ORDER SHORT EXEMPT

The first 4 situations in which a broker–dealer may mark an order short exempt are these:

1. The broker–dealer has reason to believe that the customer owns the security and will be able to deliver it as soon as all restrictions are removed.
2. A market maker has entered the order to offset a short-sale odd-lot order or to sell an odd-lot position that changes the broker–dealer's position in the security by no more than 1 unit of trading.
3. The broker–dealer is aware that the customer owns the security already and will be able to meet the delivery requirements, and the reason the customer entered into the sale is to take advantage of the difference between the current price and the price at which the customer acquired the security already in possession.
4. The broker–dealer wants to take advantage of the price discrepancy between a security offered on a foreign securities market and one offered on a national exchange, assuming the country from which the foreign security was issued permits covered short sales.

The final 3 situations in which a broker–dealer may mark an order short exempt are these:

1. The short sale is entered by an underwriter (or member of a syndicate group), and the short sale is related to an over-allotment of securities or a layoff sale.
2. A broker–dealer enters a short sale order in a riskless principal capacity, assuming the following conditions are met: The order was received before entering into the offsetting transaction; within 1 minute of the execution, the order was allocated to either a riskless principal account or the customer's account; and the broker–dealer's firm has systems in place that allow for the chronological reconstruction of events related to the order.
3. A broker–dealer enters a short sale order at the volume weighted average price (VWAP).

Accepting Short Sale Orders in a Customer Account

For a broker–dealer to accept a short sale order in a customer account, the following conditions must be met:

1. The broker–dealer already has borrowed the security or has made arrangements to do so.
2. The broker–dealer has a reasonable expectation of receiving the borrowed securities in time to comply with the delivery requirements for the security.
3. The broker–dealer has documented the specifics to demonstrate compliance with these rules.

Broker–dealers are expected to enter short-sale orders only when they have a reasonable expectation of meeting the delivery requirements. If the securities are not delivered promptly, a failure to deliver will be documented by the clearing agency. In the event that delivery does not occur within 13 days, the broker–dealer must close out the failure-to-deliver position by purchasing the same number and class of securities and delivering them immediately. The only exception to this rule is in the event that the customer already owns the securities, but there are restrictions on them that will be lifted within 35 days of the trade date, and this information has been communicated previously. After 35 days, if the securities have not been delivered, the broker–dealer must fulfill the order by purchasing the securities and delivering them immediately.

Moving an Account to Another Institution

When a customer wishes to transfer an account to another institution, the following must occur:

1. The customer completes a transfer instruction form and provides it to the broker–dealer who will receive the assets.
2. That broker–dealer will submit the transfer instruction form to the firm that is currently holding the assets.
3. The carrying firm has 1 day to validate the instructions by providing the broker–dealer with a statement reflecting all positions and balances carried in the account, at which point the carrying firm has 3 days to initiate the account transfer.
4. If the carrying firm is unable to validate the instructions, it must provide the broker–dealer with the rationale why the account cannot be transferred in its current form. Once any issues are worked through, the carrying firm has 3 business days to initiate the account transfer.

The reasons that the carrying firm may turn down a request to transfer a customer's account to another firm include the following:

1. Additional documentation is needed (death certificate, divorce decree, or marriage certificate).
2. The account does not contain any assets.
3. The account number is incorrect.

4. It is a duplicate request.
5. To transfer the account would violate the carrying firm's credit policy.
6. The customer rescinds the instruction in writing.
7. The social security number on the transfer instruction form does not match the one that the carrying firm has on file.
8. The account title on the transfer instruction form does not match the one that the carrying firm has on file.
9. The transfer instruction form is incomplete or was signed by the incorrect person.
10. The account contains proprietary assets that are not eligible for transfer.
11. The customer has taken possession of the assets in the account.

Securities That Are Excluded from the Three-Day Account Transfer Delivery Rule

The following securities are excluded from the account transfer rule requiring that a carrying firm initiate transfer of account assets within 3 days of validating the request:

1. Annuity contracts
2. Stripped coupons
3. When-issued or when-distributed securities

Securities Exchange Act Rule 10b5-1

Securities Exchange Act Rule 10b5-1 deals with the sales and purchases of securities, while an individual is in possession of material nonpublic information, whether the information is about the security itself or the company. The rule lays out the only 2 permissible defenses to a potential violation of the rule.

One of the permissible defenses is where the individual in possession of the material nonpublic information is able to prove that, before receiving or learning the information, he or she entered into an official written plan or binding contract that meets 1 of the following conditions:

1. The plan or contract specifies the exact number of shares to be transacted, the price, and the date on which the transaction is to take place.
2. The plan or contract has an algorithm or formula that, when followed, determines the exact number of shares to be transacted, the price, and the date on which the transaction is to take place.
3. The plan or contract does not allow the individual to have any control over whether the transaction takes place, including the price and the date on which the transaction is to take place.

One of the permissible defenses is when someone other than the person in possession of the material nonpublic information is making investment decisions and takes steps to ensure that his or her transaction decisions are in no way influenced by information that might be known by the account owner (e.g., the account is managed discretionarily by an investment advisor who makes the same transactions for all accounts).

Situations in Which the Issuer Is Not Required to Make Prompt Public Disclosure of Material Nonpublic Information

An issuer is not required to publicly disclose material nonpublic information that was shared with a specific person if any of the following is true:

1. The person receiving the information is in a position of confidence where a duty of trust exists (e.g., an attorney).
2. The person receiving the information is covered by a nondisclosure agreement.
3. The information is disclosed in a registration statement.
4. The information is disclosed in a free writing prospectus.

Duty of Trust

A duty of trust exists in the following circumstances:

1. When 1 party expressly agrees to keeping information privately or in confidence
2. When the party supplying material nonpublic information has an expectation of privacy due to a relationship that exists in which the regular sharing of confidential information has occurred
3. When the party receiving material nonpublic information is the spouse, parent, child, or sibling of the party supplying it, unless it can be established that there was no expectation of privacy

Underwriting Compensation

The following items are all considered to have value under the terminology of underwriting compensation:

1. Discount or commission
2. Reimbursement of expenses
3. Fees and expenses for underwriter's counsel
4. Finder's fees
5. Wholesaler's fees
6. Financial consulting and advisory fees
7. Securities, including common or preferred stock, stock options, and warrants

The following items do not count as underwriting compensation:

1. Blue sky and other registration fees, Financial Industry Regulatory Authority (FINRA) filing fees, and accountant's fees
2. Cash compensation paid for acting as a placement agent in a private placement arrangement or for providing a loan or other service in a merger or acquisition
3. Listed securities purchased in public market transactions

4. Employer securities benefits: stock bonuses, pensions, or profit-sharing plans
5. Securities acquired by a company registered under the Investment Company Act
6. Non-convertible or non-exchangeable debt securities that are purchased at fair market value in an unrelated transaction
7. Derivative investments that are purchased at fair market value in an unrelated transaction

Valuation of a Security Received as Compensation in a Public Offering

Should an underwriter (or anyone related to the underwriter) receive securities as part of his or her compensation, there must be a known valuation. The value may be determined either based on the price of an identical security offered in an independent market or by using 1 of the valuation formulas specifically permitted.

Valuation of Securities and Warrants

To determine the valuation of securities received as part of underwriting compensation where the shares do not have an exercise or conversion price, the following steps should be followed:

- Step 1: Subtract the per-share cost from the market price per share on the date of acquisition (of the market price is not known, use the public offering price).
- Step 2: Multiply the result of Step 1 by the number of shares received.
- Step 3: Divide the result from Step 2 by the offering proceeds.
- Step 4: Multiply the result from Step 3 by 100.
- Step 5: If the lock-up period is 180 days or less, stop here.
- Step 6: If the lock-up period exceeds 180 days, multiply the result from Step 4 by 90 percent (i.e., receive a 10 percent discount).

To determine the valuation of warrants received as part of underwriting compensation where the shares have an exercise or conversion price, the following steps should be followed:

- Step 1: Calculate the public offering price per share x 65 percent – exercise price – market price per share on date of acquisition (if the market price is not known, use the public offering price).
- Step 2: Divide the result from Step 1 by 2.
- Step 3: Multiply the result from Step 2 by the number of securities underlying the warrants.
- Step 4: Subtract the result from Step 3 by the total price paid for the warrants.
- Step 5: Divide the result from Step 4 by the offering proceeds.
- Step 6: Multiply the result from Step 5 by 100.

- Step 7: If the lock-up period is 180 days or less, stop here.
- Step 8: If the lock-up period exceeds 180 days, multiply the result from Step 6 by 90 percent (i.e., receive a 10 percent discount).

To determine the valuation of securities received as part of underwriting compensation where the shares do not have an exercise or conversion price, the following steps should be followed:

- Step 1: Subtract the per-share cost from the market price per share on the date of acquisition (if the market price is not known, use the public offering price).
- Step 2: Multiply the result of Step 1 by the number of shares received.
- Step 3: Divide the result from Step 2 by the offering proceeds.
- Step 4: Multiply the result from Step 3 by 100.
- Step 5: If the lock-up period is 180 days or less, stop here.
- Step 6: If the lock-up period exceeds 180 days, multiply the result from Step 4 by 90 percent (i.e., receive a 10 percent discount).

To determine the valuation of warrants received as part of underwriting compensation where the shares have an exercise or conversion price, the following steps should be followed:

- Step 1: Calculate the public offering price per share x 65 percent – exercise price – market price per share on date of acquisition (if the market price is not known, use the public offering price).
- Step 2: Divide the result from Step 1 by 2.
- Step 3: Multiply the result from Step 2 by the number of securities underlying the warrants.
- Step 4: Subtract the result from Step 3 by the total price paid for the warrants.
- Step 5: Divide the result from Step 4 by the offering proceeds.
- Step 6: Multiply the result from Step 5 by 100.
- Step 7: If the lock-up period is 180 days or less, stop here.
- Step 8: If the lock-up period exceeds 180 days, multiply the result from Step 6 by 90 percent (i.e., receive a 10 percent discount).

Prohibited Arrangements Associated with Underwriting Compensation Packages

The first 5 prohibited arrangements are these:

1. Payment for any accountable expense that the underwriter would incur during normal course of business (e.g., salaries or supplies)
2. Any nonaccountable expense that exceeds more than 3 percent of the offering proceeds

3. Payment of any compensation prior to the public sale of the securities being offered, except that which is reasonably expected to be incurred prior to the commencement of the offering
4. Any tail fee arrangement that extends more than 2 years from the date the services are terminated
5. Any first right of refusal to provide the underwriter the opportunity to underwrite future public offerings that have a duration of more than 3 years from the commencement of the offering to the public or have more than 1 opportunity to waive the right of refusal in exchange for a payment

The second set of 4 prohibited arrangements are these:

1. Payment to terminate a first right of refusal that has a value greater than 1 percent of the offering proceeds in the offering where the right was granted or is not paid in cash
2. Compensation consists of options, warrants, or convertible securities that meet any of the following criteria:
3. Is exercisable or convertible more than 5 years after the date of the offering
4. Has more than 1 demand registration right at the issuer's expense
5. Has a demand registration right with a duration of more than 5 years
6. Has a piggyback registration right with a duration of more than 7 years
7. Has antidilution terms that allow the underwriter to receive additional shares at a lower price than initially agreed upon or to receive or accrue cash dividends
8. Valuation of the compensation that cannot be determined at the time of the offering report
9. In a firm commitment basis, any over-allotment option allowing for more than 15 percent of the securities

The final 3 prohibited arrangements are these:

1. Receipt of warrants, options, convertible securities, or units containing these securities where at least 1 of the following is true:
2. The market price is lower than the exercise or conversion price.
3. The warrant, option, or convertible security is held in a discretionary account at the time of the exercise or conversion (unless the customer gives specific permission).
4. The specific compensation arrangements associated with the warrant, option, or convertible security are not disclosed in the prospectus or offering circular.
5. The exercise or conversion of the warrants, options, or convertible securities cannot be solicited by the underwriter.

6. For a member to participate with an issuer in the distribution of non-underwritten issue of securities if the issuer hired people specifically for that purpose
7. For a member to participate in a public offering of real estate investment trust securities unless the trustee discloses the information in each annual report

Financial Risk Management Controls

The financial risk management controls referenced under Securities Exchange Act (SEA) Rule 15c3-5 are intended to reduce the financial exposure a broker–dealer could experience due to his or her access to the market. In particular, these controls restrict the entry of incorrect orders by rejecting those that are duplicative or are not within certain size or price parameters. These controls can be outsourced to an outside third party; however, the broker–dealer still is responsible for ensuring the controls are implemented correctly, and the CEO of the firm must certify that the broker–dealer is in compliance on an annual basis.

Regulatory Risk Management Controls

The regulatory risk management controls referenced under Securities Exchange Act (SEA) Rule 15c3-5 are intended to confirm compliance with all requirements put forth by regulatory bodies. These controls can be outsourced to an outside third party; however, the broker–dealer still is responsible for ensuring the controls are implemented correctly, and the CEO of the firm must certify that the broker–dealer is in compliance on an annual basis.

In particular, these controls ensure the following:

1. Orders are not entered unless all regulatory requirements are met first.
2. Orders are not entered without first confirming that no parties involved are restricted in the transaction.
3. Access to trading systems and customer data are restricted only to those specifically authorized by the broker–dealer.
4. Post-trade execution reports are immediately available to the appropriate personnel.

Accrued Interest Rules Associated with When, as, and If Issued or When, as, and If Distributed Contracts

For When, As, and If Issued or When, As, and If Distributed contracts, obligations will include accrued interest up to the date of settlement unless the parties involved agreed to something different at the time of the contract. These types of contracts should be traded flat, meaning that all payments after the settlement date of the contract are considered income to the purchaser of the contract. There is 1 exception to this rule. In the case of a distribution announced prior to the settlement but paid after settlement, the distribution will be income to the seller of the contract.

Segregation of Deposits Against When, as, and If Issued or When, as, and If Distributed Contracts

In some cases, a customer may be required to make a deposit (in the form of cash or collateral) against a When, As, and If Issued or When, As, and If Distributed contract. In these instances, it is recommended that the deposits are not comingled with other cash balances so that an accurate picture of the firm's assets, liabilities, and outstanding commitments is truly understood. NASDAQ goes on to suggest that a member firm should consider depositing these funds in a bank that does not hold any of the general deposits or loans of the firm. Regardless of whether the member firm follows this particular recommendation, it is clear that utilizing deposits on these types of contracts for any purpose is prohibited.

Unlawful Activities Related to the Purchase or Sale of Securities

The unlawful activities related to the purchase or sale of securities include the following:

1. A member may mislead the public into thinking that a security is actively trading by executing transactions where there is no change in beneficial ownership.
2. A member may not execute swap or security-swap agreements in order to try to create an appearance of active trading.
3. A member may not enter orders into the system in order to fix or stabilize prices unless it is deemed necessary by the Securities & Exchange Commission.

Beneficial Owner

In general, owning greater than 10 percent of the outstanding shares of a company's stock results in being defined as an insider and being subject to certain restrictions involving the disposition of the stock. The term *beneficial owner* implies that an individual or organization owns the shares of a company's stock for the benefit of another. When this occurs, even if the aggregate number of shares held by that individual or organization exceeds 10 percent of the company's outstanding shares, the dispositive restrictions will not be enforced. An example of this concept is when a pension plan holds shares in a pool for the benefit of many employees.

Determining Investment Suitability

The following is a list of the items that a broker–dealer must know about a customer at a minimum to determine whether a particular investment is suitable:

1. Customer's age
2. Other holdings in the customer's portfolio
3. Overall financial situation (including net worth and overall income needs)
4. Tax status (bracket, filing status, state tax rate, and capital loss carryforward)
5. Investment objectives (growth, aggressive growth, income, or capital preservation)
6. Investment experience (i.e., how advanced have the holdings been in the past)

7. Investment time horizon (i.e., how long until it is necessary to pull from the portfolio as a source of cash flow)
8. Risk tolerance

Yield Calculations

Current yield illustrates the rate of return an investor would receive were he or she to purchase the bond today and hold it for 1 year. The formula is: $\frac{Annual\ Income}{Current\ Price}$

Yield to call allows the holder of a bond to calculate the yield of a bond from date of purchase until date of call. It is calculated by determining the interest rate an investor would receive were he or she to invest all coupon payments at a constant interest rate until the bond's call date.

Yield to maturity works the same way as yield to call, only the calculation takes into consideration all of the coupon payments until the bond's maturity rate.

Yield to worst is the lowest yield that a bondholder could receive without the issuer of the debt defaulting. The calculation takes into consideration a few worst-case scenarios based on the underlying provisions of the bond in question.

Bond equivalent yield is used when bonds make coupon payments more frequently than annually. It enables investors to make fair comparisons between 2 bonds that have different payment streams.

The formula is: $\frac{Par\ Value - Purchase\ Price}{Purchase\ Price} \times \frac{365}{Days\ to\ Maturity}$

Direct Participation Program (DPP)

A direct participation program (DPP) is when the tax consequences flow to a personal tax return (i.e., 1040 for an individual) regardless of the how the underlying entity is structured. For example, an individual (or married couple) who participates in an oil and gas partnership will report the tax consequences on a 1040, not on a 1065 (partnership tax return). The exceptions to this rule include real estate investment trusts (REITs) and any qualified tax-deferred accounts (individual retirement accounts [IRAs], pensions, or profit-sharing plans to name a few).

For a sales agent to purchase a direct participation program (DPP) interest for a customer, suitability must first be established. This includes the following:

1. Determine that the customer is in a financial position to understand the structure of the program, including the tax consequences.
2. Determine the customer is capable of understanding benefits of a DPP as laid out in the prospectus.
3. Determine that the customer has enough liquid assets to ensure that immediate liquidity will not be required from the DPP.

Undue Concentration

Undue concentration occurs when a customer's portfolio (not just a single account) has an unnecessarily high exposure to a single security. This is especially true if the security is not in keeping with the customer's stated investment objectives or risk tolerance. In general, an exposure to a single security should never exceed 10 percent of the value of the total portfolio. There is an exception to this rule—if the customer is an officer, director, or major shareholder (owns greater than 5 percent of the outstanding shares), the undue concentration rule may not apply. However, it is considered a best practice to have a customer sign a waiver indicating that he or she understands the inherent risk in holding a concentrated position of a single stock.

Permissible Deductions

A nonmarketable security is one that has no ready market and cannot be offered publicly due to statutory, regulatory, or other contractual agreements. If a nonmarketable security exists, a 100 percent deduction is permissible.

Brokers who have open contractual commitments that have been in failed-to-deliver status for more than 5 business days (21 business days for municipal securities) are allowed to deduct 30 percent of the value unless the underlying security is listed on a national securities exchange or is designated as a NASDAQ National Market System Security. A broker who maintains an excess of $250,000 of net capital may add back to net worth up to $150,000 of open contractual commitments.

A member firm that carries market maker accounts is allowed to take certain deductions if there are transactions in options listed on a registered national securities exchange within the account. The deductions that are permitted include any that are deficient in collateral or are under margined for a total of 5 business days or more and up to 4 percent of the indebtedness collateralized by exempted securities. For the purposes of this deduction, exempted securities are defined as those specifically referenced in the Securities Exchange Act of 1934.

Listed Option

A listed option is any option that is traded on a registered national securities exchange or by an automated facility of a registered national securities exchange. For a market maker account, the equity is computed by completing the following steps:

1. Determine the market value of all security positions in the account, both long and short.
2. Add the credit balance carried in the account.
3. Deduct the debit balance carried in the account.
4. Add the market value of the all long positions.
5. Deduct the market value of all short positions.

Ready Market

The term *ready market* means an established securities market in which independent, bona-fide offers to buy and sell at reasonable prices exist. The bid and offer quotations must be competitive and available nearly instantaneously. The payment for any security purchase must be received within a short period of time, and delivery of the security must meet all regulatory protocols. A ready market is also said to exist when securities have been accepted by a bank as collateral for a loan and the broker–dealer is able to demonstrate that he or she adequately secured the loan.

Principal Regulator

The term *principal regulator* is someone who is not a registered broker or dealer and is 1 of the following:

1. An insured depository institution
2. A futures commission merchant
3. Introducing broker with the Commodity Futures Trading Commission
4. Licensed by a state insurance regulator
5. A foreign bank
6. Not primarily in the securities business and a corporation organized under Section 25A of the Federal Reserve Act

An ultimate holding company that has a principal regulator is a financial holding company or a company that is treated as a financial holding company under the Bank Holding Company Act of 1956, or the Securities & Exchange Commission (SEC) determines that the company meets the requirements to be an ultimate holding company, and there is consolidated comprehensive supervision in place.

Tentative Net Capital

Tentative net capital is the net capital of a broker–dealer before he or she takes any permissible deductions, including securities haircuts. The term also means the net capital of an over-the-counter (OTC) derivatives dealer before deducting the charges for market and credit risk. Tentative net capital does include securities for which there is no ready market.

Debt-Equity Requirements

A broker–dealer is not allowed to permit the total outstanding principal amounts to exceed 70 percent of his or her debt-equity total for a period longer than 90 days. The Securities & Exchange Commission (SEC) may make exceptions to this rule on a case-by-case basis but only if it is in the best interest of the customers of a broker–dealer. Debt equity is considered to be the sum of the following:

1. Outstanding principal amounts
2. Par or stated value of capital stock
3. Paid in capital in excess of par
4. Retained earnings

5. Unrealized profit and loss
6. Other capital accounts

Withdrawal of Equity Capital

If a withdrawal is greater than $500,000 and equal to more than 30 percent of a broker–dealer's net capital, advance notice must be given (and approval made) by its examining authority. This is true whether the withdrawal is in the form of an unsecured loan against the company, in the form of a withdrawal of cash, by redemption or repurchase of shares of stock or through the payment of dividends, or through other similar distribution. If the amount of the withdrawal is greater than $500,000 and represents between 20 and 30 percent of the net capital, advance notice is not required, but the examining authority must be notified within 2 business days of the withdrawal taking place.

Fidelity Bonds

The general provisions of a fidelity bond include blanket coverage and must include at a minimum the following:

1. Fidelity
2. On premises
3. In transit
4. Forgery and alteration
5. Securities
6. Counterfeit currency
7. Cancellation rider
8. Per loss coverage without an aggregate limit of liability

A member with a net capital requirement less than $250,000 must maintain a fidelity bond insuring the greater of 120 percent of its net capital or $100,000. If a member has greater than a $250,000 net capital requirement, the minimum coverage is based on the chart below.

Net Capital Requirement	Minimum Coverage
$250,000–$350,000	$600,000
$300,001–$500,000	$700,000
$500,001–$1,000,000	$800,000
$1,000,001–$2,000,000	$1,000,000
$2,000,001–$3,000,000	$1,500,000
$3,000,001–$4,000,000	$2,000,000
$4,000,001–$6,000,000	$3,000,000
$6,000,001–$12,000,000	$4,000,000
Greater than $12,000,000	$5,000,000

FINRA's Capital Compliance Regulations

The Financial Industry Regulatory Authority's (FINRA's) capital compliance regulations state that, in its discretion, it may require a higher net capital requirement for any firm. A member that is not in compliance with FINRA capital regulations must seek approval to continue its business operations. A firm that knowingly is not in compliance with these regulations may be subject to strict penalties, including the loss of earned profits during the time period it was not in compliance.

Restrictions to Business Expansion

Unless given express permission by Financial Industry Regulatory Authority (FINRA), if a member is not meeting its net minimum capital requirements, it may not expand its business. Expanding its business includes the following:

1. A net increase in the number of registered representatives
2. Exceeding average capital commitments over the previous 3 months for market making or block positioning
3. Initiation of market making in new securities
4. Exceeding average commitments over the previous 3 months for underwriting
5. Opening new branch offices
6. Entering a new line of business
7. Making unsecured or only partially secured loans

Rights the FINRA Has to Audit a Member Firm's Financial Statements

The Financial Industry Regulatory Authority (FINRA) has the right to request a firm's financial statements, books, records, or prior audited financial statements if it has concerns about the accuracy or integrity of them. The audit will be requested by FINRA's executive vice president or a written delegate to the executive vice president. If a member fails to provide the requested information in a timely fashion, he or she may be subject to a late fee.

Transaction Reporting Requirements

Brokers, dealers, and municipal securities dealers are required to report to the board information about each purchase and sale of municipal securities to the Real-Time Transaction Reporting System (RTRS). The information collected under this rule is used to make public reports about market activity, prices charged, and transaction fees assessed. It allows the board to ensure that the board rules are being followed and identify and be in contact with members who are not in full compliance. There are a few securities that are not subject to the reporting requirements including those that do not have assigned Committee on Uniform Securities Identification Procedures (CUSIP) numbers, municipal funds, and those interdealer transactions (i.e., the movement of the securities are not eligible for comparison in a clearing agency).

Official Statement That Underwriters of Municipal Securities Are Required to Make

Under Rule G-32, underwriters of a primary offering of municipal securities are required to send an official statement to Electronic Municipal Market Access (EMMA) within 1 business day after receipt of the statement from the issuer. If the official statement is not submitted by the underwriter by the closing date, the underwriter must submit to EMMA the following information:

1. The date that the official statement will be available and a commitment to send it when available
2. The preliminary official statement and a commitment to send the official statement when available
3. The fact that no official statement has been prepared because it is an exempt offering

Records That Every Broker–Dealer Is Required to Keep

The first 3 records that every broker–dealer is required to keep according to Rule G-8 are these:

1. Records of original entry—this is an itemized daily record of all purchases and sales of municipal securities
2. Account records—these are records for each customer account that reflect all purchases and sales of municipal securities
3. Securities records—this is a list of each municipal security that is held within a customer account

The second set of 3 records that every broker–dealer is required to keep according to Rule G-8 include the following:

1. Subsidiary records—this is a listing of any municipal securities that are currently being transferred, borrowed, or loaned
2. Put options and repurchase agreements, both written or oral records for agency transactions—this is a written memo that shows the terms and conditions of any municipal transactions done on an agency basis

The third set of 3 records that every broker–dealer is required to keep according to Rule G-8 include the following:

1. Records for principal transactions—this is a written memo that shows the terms and conditions of any municipal transactions done on a principal basis
2. Records concerning primary offerings—this is a record showing the name and participation level of each member in a syndicate
3. Copies of confirmation statements

The final 2 records that every broker–dealer is required to keep according to Rule G-8 include the following:

1. Financial records in keeping with the Securities Exchange Act
2. Customer account information including name, social security number (or tax identification number), address, whether the customer is of legal age, occupation, name and address of employer, and the name of any beneficial owner

PRE-DISPUTE ARBITRATION RULES THAT BOTH CUSTOMERS AND BROKERS AGREE TO AT THE TIME THEY SIGN THE AGREEMENT

The pre-dispute arbitration rules are for both customers and brokers and include the following:

1. All parties are giving up the right to sue in court and agree to arbitration forums.
2. The arbitration awards are final and binding.
3. The ability to obtain documents, witness statements, and other discovery documents are more limited than in a typical court proceeding.
4. The arbitrators do not have to explain the basis for their decision.
5. The panel of arbitrators typically will include a minority of arbitrators who were or are affiliated with the securities industry.

RECORDS THAT BROKERS TRADING IN MUNICIPAL SECURITIES MUST KEEP CONCERNING THEIR POLITICAL CONTRIBUTIONS

The first 4 records that brokers trading in municipal securities must keep concerning their political contributions are these:

1. A listing of the names, titles, city, county, and state of all municipal finance professionals
2. A listing of the names, titles, city, county, and state of all nonmunicipal finance professional executive officers
3. The states in which the broker is engaging or is seeking to engage in municipal securities business
4. A listing of issuers with which the broker has engaged in municipal securities business, along with the type of securities during the current year and a separate list for the prior 2 years

The second set of 4 records that brokers trading in municipal securities must keep concerning their political contributions are these:

1. The contributions a broker makes to officials of an issuer, payments made to the political parties of states and political subdivisions for the current year, and a separate list for the prior 2 years
2. The contributions of each municipal finance professional made to officials of an issuer or any political action committee controlled by a municipal finance professional for the current year and a separate list for the prior 2 years
3. The contributions to political parties of states and political subdivisions made by all nonmunicipal finance professional executive officers and any political action committee controlled by a nonmunicipal finance professional executive officer for the current year and a separate list for the 2 prior years
4. The contributions to bond ballot campaigns made by the broker in the current year and a separate list for the 2 prior years

The last 2 records that brokers trading in municipal securities must keep concerning their political contributions are these:

1. The contributions to bond ballot campaigns by each nonmunicipal finance professional executive officer for the current year and a separate list for the 2 prior years
2. Copies of the Forms G-37 and G-37X

Information That Must Be Included on a Dealer's Confirmation Statement

The first 6 pieces of information that must be included on a dealer's confirmation statement are these:

1. Confirming party's name, address, and telephone number
2. Contra-party identification
3. Designation of purchase from or sale to
4. Par value of securities
5. Description of the securities, including the name of the issuer, the interest rate, maturity date, and if the securities are subject to taxation
6. Committee on Uniform Securities Identification Procedures (CUSIP) number

The final 8 pieces of information that must be included on a dealer's confirmation statement include the following:

1. Trade date
2. Settlement date
3. Yield at which the transaction was effected and resulting dollar price
4. Amount of concession, if any, per $1,000 par value
5. Amount of accrued interest
6. Extended principal amount
7. Total dollar amount of transaction
8. Instructions regarding receipt or delivery of securities and form of payment

Process That Should Be Followed If the Dealer Confirmation Statement Does Not Match Up with the Transaction Details

If either party to a transaction believes that the confirmation statement does not match up with the transaction details, they should communicate the discrepancies to the other party, and both parties should work together to resolve the discrepancy. The party in error has 1 business day to send a corrected confirmation. Upon receipt, the party receiving the corrected confirmation should review the statement for accuracy and acknowledge that it is updated and correct.

Process of Security Delivery

The following provisions must be observed related to the delivery of a security:

1. The Committee on Uniform Securities Identification Procedures (CUSIP) numbers must match what is reflected on the confirmation statement.
2. The securities delivered must have the same call provisions and date as what is reflected on the confirmation statement.
3. Partial delivery does not have to be accepted.
4. The units of delivery must be in denominations of $1,000 or $5,000 par value for bearer bonds.
5. The units of delivery must be in multiples of $1,000 par value up to $100,000 for registered bonds.

Scenarios in Which a Certificate Will Be Considered Mutilated

A certificate will be considered mutilated if any of the following information is not ascertainable:

1. Name of issuer
2. Par value
3. Signature
4. Coupon rate
5. Maturity date
6. Seal of the issuer
7. Certificate number

Monetary Differences That Would Be Great Enough to Cause Rejection of Security Delivery

The following money differences would cause rejection of a security delivery:

Par Value	Maximum Difference Per Transaction
$1,000–$24,999	$10
$25,000–$99,999	$25
$100,000–$249,999	$60
$250,000–$999,999	$250
$1,000,000 and greater	$500

Reasons That a Security May Be Rejected and the Time Frame in Which It Must Be Done

Depending upon what is wrong with a security, there are time limits in which a broker must reject the security. In general, the time limits are either 1 day or 18 months. The things that fall in the 1-day category include the following:

1. Missing a coupon or interest check
2. Mutilated coupon
3. Missing legal opinion

The things that fall into the 18-months category include the following:

1. Irregularity in delivery, including the delivery of the wrong security, to the wrong location or the wrong party
2. Refusal to transfer or deregister by the transfer agent due because it is missing documentation
3. Inaccurate or incomplete description of the securities

Reclamation of a Security

There are no time limits for reclamation demands; however, they can be made only for the following reasons:

1. The security delivered was reported previously as missing, stolen, or counterfeit.
2. The security delivered was called (i.e., a call feature was enacted) previously but was not recorded properly.
3. The issuer calls the security on the day of the transaction, before the trade is recorded, and the fact that the security had been called was not made known to the purchaser.

Information Included in the Written Notice That a Rejecting or Reclaiming Party Provides

In order to reject or reclaim a security, written notice must be provided (for rejections, it must be provided within the allowable time frames). This notice must have the original delivery ticket and proof of delivery attached to it and list the following information:

1. The name of the party delivering the securities
2. The name of the party receiving the securities
3. A description of the securities
4. The date the securities were delivered
5. The date of rejection or reclamation
6. The par value of the securities
7. The amount of money the securities are reclaimed for (if applicable)
8. The reason for the rejection or reclamation
9. Name and telephone number of the person to contact regarding the rejection or reclamation

Notice of Closeout

The first 5 pieces of information that must be included in the notice of closeout to be in keeping with Rule G-12 include the following:

1. The name of the broker, dealer, or municipal securities dealer who is originating the notice as well as his or her address
2. The name of the broker, dealer, or municipal securities dealer who is receiving the notice as well as his or her address

3. Name of the person to whom the originator provided the required telephone notice
4. The date and time that the originator made the required telephone notice
5. The par value and description of the securities involved in the transaction

The final 6 pieces of information that must be included in the notice of closeout to be in keeping with Rule G-12 include the following:

1. The trade date of the transaction and the settlement date for the transaction
2. The price per security and total dollar amount of the transaction
3. The date the securities must be received by the originating dealer
4. The date or dates during which the notice of closeout is permitted to be executed
5. Whether the notice is a re-transmittal (i.e., the first notice was not properly received and is being resent)
6. Whether the notice is part of an extension (i.e., the person filing the notice requested an extension in order to gather all necessary information)

Real-Time Transaction Reporting System (RTRS) Procedures

The Real-Time Transaction Reporting System (RTRS) portal is used as follows:

1. The message-based trade input operated by National Securities Clearing Corporation (NSCC) is used for the recording or modification of trade information.
2. The NSCC RTRS can be used only for submitting or modifying data for interdealer transactions that are eligible for comparison.
3. Transactions must be entered within 15 minutes of the time of trade with a few exceptions:
4. The dealer reports an away-from-market trade.
5. The dealer reports by the end of the day that the trade becomes available for comparison by a clearing agency.
6. Trades that are not made during normal business hours can be made within 15 minutes of the start of the following business day.

Delivery Requirements

When making delivery of securities, broker–dealers need to consider the following information:

1. All securities must be identical to the information in the quotation, including call provisions and the maturity date of the securities.
2. The securities must have the same Committee on Uniform Securities Identification Procedures (CUSIP) number as those displayed on the confirmation statement.
3. A delivery ticket must accompany the securities.
4. Bearer bonds must be in denominations of $1,000 or $5,000 par value.
5. Registered bonds must be in multiples of $1,000 par value up to $100,000.
6. Delivery must be made in book-entry form.

7. Mutilated certificates are not permissible.
8. Delivery must include legal opinions.

Customer Confirmation Statements

The following information must be included on all customer confirmation statements according to Rule G-15:

1. The name, address, and telephone number of the broker, dealer, or municipal securities dealer
2. The name of the customer
3. A designation as to whether the transaction was a purchase from the customer or a sale to the customer
4. The capacity in which the broker, dealer, or municipal securities dealer that effected the transaction: a principal for its own account, an agent for the customer, an agent for a person other than the customer, or an agent for both the customer and another person
5. Trade date and time of execution
6. Par value
7. Settlement date
8. Yield and dollar price
9. Total amount of the transaction
10. Information about the delivery of the securities

Ensuring That Payments Are Handled as Efficiently as Possible

Broker-dealers must take into consideration the following things in Rule G-15:

1. The name and address of the agent and customer account number must be on file at the time an order was accepted.
2. A memo of each order needs to be created so that the broker can update it as to whether delivery or payment occurred or if there is a failed-to-deliver or failed-to-receive issue.
3. The broker–dealer must give the customer a confirmation statement no later than the day of the execution.
4. The broker–dealer must obtain information about how the customer will pay for the securities or deliver the securities to the counterparty.

Prohibition on Soliciting and Coordinating Contributions

According to Rule G-37, brokers, dealers, and municipal securities dealers are not allowed to engage in municipal securities business with an issuer within 2 years of any contribution to an official of the issuer made by any of the following:

1. The broker, dealer, or municipal securities dealer
2. Any municipal finance professional associated with the broker, dealer, or municipal securities dealer
3. Any political action committee controlled by the broker, dealer, or municipal securities dealer

In addition, brokers, dealers, and municipal securities dealers are not allowed to make a contribution or coordinate contributions to the official of an issuer in an attempt to engage in business with him or her.

Form G-37

Quarterly (January 31, April 30, July 31, and October 31), each broker, dealer, or municipal securities dealer must send Form G-37 to the board. The form will include the following information:

1. The name and title of each official of an issuer and political party receiving contributions or payments during the calendar quarter, listed by state
2. The contribution or payment amount made to any political organization, political party, and bond ballot campaign contributor category for the following individuals: broker, dealer, or municipal securities dealer; municipal finance professional; nonmunicipal finance professional executive officer; and each political action committee controlled by any of those mentioned in this list
3. A list of issuers that the broker, dealer, or municipal securities dealer engaged with during the quarter

Customer Disclosure

Customer disclosure will be met under the following situations:

1. The offered municipal securities are not municipal fund securities.
2. The underwriter has made the submissions to Electronic Municipal Market Access (EMMA, the municipal securities rule-making board).
3. A copy of the official statement includes the underwriting spread, the amount of the fee received by the broker as agent for the issuer, and the initial offering price for each maturity in the offering.
4. A notice is sent to the customer advising how to obtain an official statement from EMMA.

Committee on Uniform Securities Identification Procedures (CUSIP) Application Process

When the underwriter finalizes pricing information for a new issue, a written request for a Committee on Uniform Securities Identification Procedures (CUSIP) may be filed. The information that must be provided include the following:

1. Complete name of the issues and, if applicable, the series designation
2. Interest rate and maturity date (if the interest rate has not been determined yet, the application should reference that it will be provided when available)
3. Dated date
4. Type of issue (e.g., general obligation, limited tax, revenue bond)
5. Type of revenue (if applicable)
6. Details of all redemptive provisions

7. The name of the company or other person with respect to the debt service on all or part of the issue
8. Any distinction in the security or source of payment of the debt service on the issue

Application Process of Depository Eligibility

To apply for depository eligibility, each underwriter must complete the following, the underwriter must apply to a securities depository that is registered with the Securities & Exchange Commission (SEC) to make a new issue depository eligible. The application must be received no later than 1 business day after execution of the contract to purchase securities from the issuer. In the event that full documentation is not available at the time of the application, the underwriter must forward it as soon as it is available.

This rule does not apply to the following:

1. An issue of municipal securities that fails to meet the criteria for depository eligibility at all depositories that accept municipal securities for deposit.
2. A new issue that matures in 60 days or less

SHORT System

The SHORT system is the short-term obligation rate transparency system. It is used for auction rate securities that are municipal securities in which interest rates reset on a periodic basis under an auction process conducted by the agent. The following information about the auction rate security is reported through it:

- Committee on Uniform Securities Identification Procedures (CUSIP) number
- Interest rate produced by the auction process
- Identity of all program dealers that submitted orders
- Date and time of the auction
- Length of time that the interest rate is applicable
- Minimum denomination
- Minimum and maximum rates applicable at the time of the auction process (if applicable)
- Date and time the interest rate determined was communicated to the program dealers
- Aggregate par amount of orders to sell at any interest rate and the date they were executed
- Interest rates and aggregate par amounts of orders to hold at specific interest rates and aggregate par amounts that were successfully held
- Interest rates to buy and aggregate par amounts that were executed
- Interest rates, aggregate par amounts, and types of orders (buy, sell, or hold) for a program dealer's own account

Determining Accrued Interest

According to Rule 33, accrued interest must be computed based on a specific formula:

$$Interest\ Rate\ \times Par\ Value\ of\ Transaction\ \times \frac{Number\ of\ Days}{Number\ of\ Days\ in\ Year}$$

In this calculation, number of days is the number of days between the previous interest payment date up to (and including) the settlement date.

Computing the Dollar Price for a Transaction in a Security That Pays Interest Only at Redemption

The dollar price for a transaction in a security paying interest solely at redemption (i.e., zero coupon bond) is computed according to the following formula:

$$P = \left[\frac{RV + \left(\frac{DIR}{B} \times R\right)}{1 + \left(\frac{DIR - A}{B} \times Y\right)}\right] - \left[\frac{A}{B} \times R\right]$$

A = number of accrued days between the beginning of the interest payment period to the settlement date

B = number of days in the year

DIR = number of days from the issue date to the redemption date

P = dollar price for each $100 par value

R = annual interest rate

RV = redemption value of the security per $100 par value

Y = yield price of the transaction

Computing the Dollar Price for a Transaction with Periodic Interest Payments (When the Number of Months Until Redemption Is 6 or Less)

The formula for the dollar price for a transaction with period interest payments (when the number of months until redemption is 6 or less) is computed as follows:

$$P = \left[\frac{\frac{RV}{100} + \frac{R}{M}}{1 + \left(\frac{E - A}{E} \times \frac{Y}{M}\right)}\right] - \left[\frac{A}{B} \times R\right]$$

A = number of accrued days between the beginning of the interest payment period to the settlement date

B = number of days in the year

E = number of days in the interest payment period

M = number of interest payment periods for the year

P = dollar price for each $100 par value

R = annual interest rate

RV = redemption value of the security per $100 par value

Y = yield price of the transaction

Computing the Dollar Price for a Transaction with Periodic Interest Payments (When the Number of Months Until Redemption Is Greater Than 6)

The formula for the dollar price for a transaction with period interest payments (when the number of months until redemption is greater than 6) is computed as follows:

$$P = \left[\frac{RV}{\left(1+\frac{Y}{2}\right)^{N-1+\frac{E-A}{E}}}\right] + \left[\sum_{K=1}^{N} \frac{100 \times \frac{R}{2}}{\left(1+\frac{Y}{2}\right)^{K-1+\frac{E-A}{E}}}\right] - \left[100 \times \frac{A}{B} \times R\right]$$

A = number of accrued days between the beginning of the interest payment period and the settlement date

B = number of days in the year

E = number of days in the interest payment period

N = number of interest payments occurring between the settlement date and the redemption date

P = dollar price for each $100 par value

R = annual interest rate

RV = redemption value of the security per $100 par value

Y = yield price of the transaction

Computing the Dollar Price for a Discounted Security

The formula for the dollar price of a discounted security is as follows:

$$P = [RV] - \left[DR \times RV \times \frac{DSM}{B}\right]$$

B = number of days in the year

DR = discount rate

DSM = number of days from the settlement date to the maturity date

P = dollar price of the security for each $100 par value

RV = redemption value of the security per $100 par value

Calculating Return on Investment

Return on investment is calculated according to the following formula:

$$IR = \left[\frac{RV - P}{P}\right] \times \left[\frac{B}{DSM}\right]$$

B = number of days in the year

DSM = number of days from the settlement date to the maturity date

IR = annual return on investment if the security is held to maturity

P = dollar price of the security for each $100 par value

RV = redemption value of the security per $100 par value

Standards of Accuracy That Ensure Price Calculations Are Computed with the Same Level of Consistency

The following standards of accuracy must be used when calculating price calculations to ensure that customers are able to compare securities in a fair and honest way:

1. Accrued interest should be truncated to 3 decimal places and then rounded to 2 decimal places for presentation on the confirmation statement.
2. Dollar prices should be truncated to 3 decimal places immediately prior to presentation on the confirmation statement and computation of extended principal.
3. Yields should be truncated to 4 decimal places and rounded to 3 decimal places provided that for purposes of confirmation display, yields accurate to the nearest 0.05 percent are deemed to be accurate.

Dates of Delivery

Cash delivery is when the delivery of the security must occur at the office of the purchaser on the date the cash payment is received.

Regular way is when the delivery of the security must occur at the office of the purchaser on, but not before, the next business day following the execution of the transaction (T+1).

Seller's option is when the seller has some flexibility. The delivery must occur at the office of the purchaser, but the actual date of delivery can take place on any business day after the third business day following the transaction up to the date on which the option expires. The seller must provide written notice to deliver 1 business day prior to delivery.

Buyer's option is when the delivery of the security must occur at the office of the purchaser on the date the option expires. If the option expires on a weekend or a holiday, the security will be delivered on the following business day.

Glossary

Offered Municipal Securities

The term *offered municipal securities* means that municipal securities are being sold by a broker, dealer, or municipal securities dealer during the primary offering disclosure period, including those reoffered in a remarketing that constitutes a primary offering.

Official Statement

The term *official statement* is a document prepared by the issuer (or on his or her behalf if he or she hires another firm to do it) that is complete as of the date delivered to the underwriter. It provides information concerning the terms of the proposed offering of securities. A notice of sale is not the same thing as an official statement.

Primary Offering Disclosure Period

The term *primary offering disclosure period* is the period beginning with the first submission to an underwriter of an order for the purchase of offered municipal securities or the purchase of the securities from the issuer, whichever occurs first and ending 25 days after the final delivery by the issuer or its agent of all securities of the issue.

Customer Protection

Hypothecation

Hypothecation is the borrowing or pledging of an asset as collateral for a loan while still enjoying the benefits of ownership. Hypothecation usually relates to securities in a margin account that the customer uses as collateral to borrow funds while still being able to receive dividends, interest, and capital distributions.

The general restrictions for hypothecation of a customer's securities include the following:

1. A member may not arrange for or permit the continued hypothecation of securities that are comingled with another customer's account.
2. A member may not arrange for or permit the continued hypothecation of securities that are used for a loan made to the member.
3. A member may not arrange for or permit the continued hypothecation of securities when the aggregate indebtedness exceeds the value of a customer's assets.

Exemptions to the hypothecation restriction rules include the following:

1. Cash accounts
2. Liens made against securities that exceed the aggregate indebtedness rule when the repayment will occur on the same calendar day

General Prohibited Representations That Exist with the Offer of All-or-None Securities

The general prohibited representations that exist when offering all-or-none securities are these:

1. If a security is being offered on an all-or-none basis, the customer must be refunded his or her deposit promptly if the offering does not take place.
2. If a security is being offered on an all-or-none basis, the customer must be delivered his or her securities as soon as reasonably possible if the offering goes through.

Customer Confirmation Statement

The following information is required on a customer confirmation statement:

1. The date and time of the transaction
2. Whether the broker is acting as an agent or a principal
3. The name and person from whom the security is purchased
4. The amount of the remuneration
5. The source of the remuneration

Disclosures a Broker Is Required to Make If Acting as Principal for His or Her Own Account

There are specific disclosures a broker is required to make if acting as principal for his or her own account, including the following:

1. Whether any odd-lot fee was paid by the customer
2. If the redemption could affect the yield represented

Physical Possession of Securities

A broker must promptly obtain and thereafter maintain the possession or control of all fully paid securities and excess margin securities. A broker will be violation of this rule if the broker is not in control of the securities and does not take steps to take possession of them. The burden of proof is on the broker to prove that any lag time is temporary and a result of normal business operations. A broker also will be in violation of these rules if they are not fully in possession of hypothecate securities.

Valid Repurchase Agreement

For a valid repurchase agreement to be in place, it must have the following characteristics:

1. Be in writing
2. Confirm the specific securities that are subject to the repurchase agreement
3. Advise the counterparty that Securities Investor Protection Corporation (SIPC) has taken the position that the Securities Investor Protection Act (SIPA) does not protect repurchase agreements
4. Maintain possession of the securities

Reserve Bank Account Computation Rules

The reserve bank account computation rules state that the amount required to be deposited into the Customer Reserve Bank Account and PAB Reserve Bank Account must be made weekly as of the close of the last business day of the week. Any deposit made within 1 hour after the opening of the second business day will not be considered late so long as aggregate indebtedness is not in excess of 800 percent.

A broker is allowed to make withdrawals from the reserve bank account if at the time of the withdrawal the remaining amount in the account is not less than the required amount. On the day a broker makes the withdrawal, he or she is required to make a record of the computation on the basis of which he or she made the withdrawal as proof that the reserve bank account computation rules were not violated, and this computation must be preserved.

Free Credit Balance

The term *free credit balance* refers to the amount of cash held in a margin account that can be withdrawn by the customer free of restrictions. This balance is calculated as the total remaining balance after taking into consideration margin requirements and short sale proceeds. A broker is not permitted to use the free credit balance unless he or she has an established procedure that account statements are sent out at least every 3 months and include a statement as to the fact that available funds are available upon request. A broker is allowed to invest or transfer to another account or institution the free credit balances in a customer's account. He or she also may deposit these balances into sweep programs.

Regulation S-P

Securities & Exchange Commission (SEC) Regulation S-P deals with the treatment of nonpublic personal information about customers. The regulation requires that member firms notify customers about how their personal information will be used and give customers an opportunity to opt out of any sharing of their personal information. The following are examples of notices that customers might receive under Regulation S-P:

1. Initial privacy notices
2. Annual privacy notices
3. Information in privacy notices
4. Opportunity for customers to opt out
5. Revised privacy notices
6. Delivery of privacy and opt-out notices
7. Current safeguard requirements

Quarterly Security Counts

The exemptions to the requirement that members must conduct quarterly security counts are these:

1. Dealer transactions as principal for the member's own account limited to the purchase, sale, and redemption of shares of registered investment companies
2. Agent transactions limited to the sale and redemption of registered investment companies
3. The solicitation of share accounts for savings and loan associations
4. The sale of securities to obtain funds for immediate reinvestment in shares of registered investment companies
5. All funds promptly transmitted and all securities delivered to customers

Separate Customer Requirement

According to Securities Investor Protection Corporation (SIPC), to identify ownership adequately, customer accounts cannot be comingled. This rule applies specifically to the following:

1. Individual accounts
2. Estate accounts
3. Decedent accounts
4. Uniform Gifts to Minors Act (UGMA) accounts
5. Corporate accounts
6. Trust accounts

Alternative Standard

Broker–dealers may choose not to be subject to the aggregate indebtedness standard. To do this, they must contact the examining authority and actively make this election. They will follow an alternative standard that states that the broker–dealer may not allow his or her net capital to be less than the greater of the following:

1. $250,000
2. 2 percent of the aggregate debit items computed in the determination of reserve requirements formula

Determination of Reserve Requirements Formula

The determination of reserve requirements formula is used by broker–dealers who choose not to follow the aggregate indebtedness standard. The following information must be taken into the consideration:

1. The computation must be done on a weekly basis.
2. Market value for items more than 7 business days old must be included.
3. Credit balances for securities not yet received from the issuer should be excluded.
4. A deduction equal to 1 percent of the contract value for all failed-to-deliver contracts should be taken.

Deductions That Are Permitted for Unsecured Receivables

Members are permitted to deduct deficits in customer accounts once they have been outstanding for at least 5 business days. In addition, interest receivable, floor brokerage receivable, commissions receivable, and any receivables outstanding longer than 30 days from the date they arose may be deducted. For receivables from municipalities, the time frame increases to 60 days.

Documents an Underwriter Is Required to File

An underwriter is required to file the following with the Financial Industry Regulatory Authority (FINRA):

1. Registration statement
2. Offering circular
3. Offering memorandum
4. Notification of filing
5. Notice of intention
6. Application for conversion
7. Proposed underwriting agreements
8. Agreement under underwriters
9. Selected dealer agreement
10. Agency agreement
11. Purchase agreement
12. Letter of intent
13. Consulting agreement

14. Partnership agreement
15. Underwriter's warrant agreement
16. Escrow agreement

Regulation T

Regulation T is the policy that dictates the amount of credit a broker–dealer can extend to a customer. The policy is made by the Federal Reserve Board and provides for rules based on the type of assets held in a customer's account. In general, a customer may borrow up to 50 percent of the purchase price of a security. This is known as buying on margin. Regulation T goes on to define when a customer is overextended and how a broker–dealer must handle these situations.

According to Regulation T, permissible transactions in a cash account include the following:

1. The ability to buy or sell to any customer any security or other asset if there are sufficient funds or the creditor accepts on good faith that the customer promptly will deposit the funds necessary to complete the transaction
2. The ability to buy or sell for any customer if the security is held in the account or the creditor accepts good faith that the customer promptly will deposit the security in the account
3. Issue, endorsement, or guarantee an option for a customer as part of a covered option transaction
4. Use of an escrow agreement in lieu of cash if, in the case of a short call or short put, the creditor is advised that the required assets or cash will be deposited promptly

A creditor may borrow or lend securities in the case of short sales, failure to receive securities required to be delivered, or other similar instances. If a creditor anticipates that 1 of these situations is going to occur, the borrowing may be made up to 1 standard settlement cycle in advance of the trade date. A creditor may lend foreign securities to a foreign person if it is in keeping with the laws of the country in which they will be used.

Glossary

Failed to Receive

Failed to receive means that 1 party failed to pay to another the contract price in cash upon receipt of the securities purchased as part of a contractual commitment.

Failed to Deliver

Failed to deliver means that 1 party failed to deliver the securities upon receipt of the contract price as part of a contractual commitment.

Open Contractual Commitment

Open contractual commitment means that a failed to receive or a failed to deliver within 3 business days has occurred and that, as a result, the contractual commitment is still open.

Financial Reporting Requirements

Disclosure Requirements That Exist When a Member Enters into Contract with an Issuer

When a member enters into contract with an issuer, the member is required to disclose to customers that the relationship exists as well as any compensation arrangement that may exist. If the disclosure is given to customers orally, then it must be followed up as a supplemental disclosure at or before the completion of the first transaction related to any security of that issuer.

Situations Which Require Reporting Within 30 Days of the Event Occurring

The following situations require filing a report with the Financial Industry Regulatory Authority (FINRA) within 30 days of the event:

1. Someone associated with the member has been found to have violated a securities, insurance, commodities, financial, or investment-related rule or standard of conduct.
2. Someone associated with the member is subject to a written complaint about the theft or misappropriations of funds.
3. Someone associated with the member is named as a defendant in a suit alleging a violation of the Securities Exchange Act.
4. Someone associated with the member is denied registration or expelled from a securities, insurance, or commodities regulatory firm or association.
5. Someone associated with the member is indicted, convicted of, or pleads guilty to a felony or any security-related misdemeanor.
6. Someone associated with the member is a defendant or respondent in a securities- or commodities-related civil litigation or arbitration where the award could exceed $15,000.
7. Someone associated with the member is subject to a disciplinary action involving suspension, termination, or withholding of compensation in excess of $2,500.

Furnishing Recent Financial Statements to Other Members

Disclosure of financial condition (FINRA Rule 2261) - a member is required to furnish recent financial statements to other members upon request when the member is party to an open transaction or has on deposit cash or securities of another member.

Monthly and Quarterly Reports That Have to Be Filed

Every broker or dealer that clears or carries customer accounts is to file:

- Part 1 of Form X-17A-5 within ten business after the end of each month; and
- Part 2 of Form X-17A-5 within 17 business days after the end of each quarter and within 17 business days after the annual audit of financial statements.

- Every broker or dealer who does not clear or carry customer accounts is to file Part 2A of Form X-17A-5 within 17 business days after the end of each quarter and within 17 business days after the annual audit of financial statements.
- Certain brokers or dealers who calculate their capital charges according to Rule 15c3-1e must file additional reports.

Report to Be Filed Upon Termination of Membership and Customer Statements

Report filed upon termination of membership interest - if a broker or dealer with a membership in a national securities exchange or registered national securities association is no longer in good standing, the broker or dealer is—within two days of the event—to file Part 2 and Part 2A of Form X-17A-5 with the SEC.

Customer statements - every broker or dealer is to send to his customers, and file with the SEC, the following unaudited statements within 65 days of the date of the statement: balance sheet, a net capital statement footnote, and a statement of availability of the Statement of Financial Condition. For purposes of this rule, the term "customer" means any person who is not a broker, dealer, partner or officer of a broker or dealer, or certain persons with claim to the capital of a broker or dealer.

Annual Filing of Audited Financial Statements, Qualification of Accountants, and Audit Objectives

Annual filing of audited financial statements - annually a broker or dealer is to file a report that has been audited by an independent public accountant. This report is to contain a Statement of Financial Condition, a Statement of Income, a Statement of Cash Flows, a Statement of Changes in Stockholders' Equity, and a Statement of Changes in Liabilities Subordinated to Claims of General Creditors.

Qualification of accountants - in order to be recognized by the Commission, an accountant must be registered, in good standing, and entitled to practice.

Audit objectives - the audit should following generally accepted auditing standards, and is to include audits of the accounting system, the internal accounting control, and procedures for safeguarding securities.

Technical Requirements, Representations as to the Audit, and Opinion to Be Expressed

Technical requirements - the accountant's report is to be dated and manually signed. It is to indicate the city and state and detail the financial statements and schedules covered by the report.

Representations as to the audit - the report shall state whether the audit followed generally accepted auditing standards; state whether the accountant reviewed the procedures for safeguarding securities; and designate auditing procedures deemed necessary that have been omitted and why.

Opinion to be expressed - the report is to clearly state the opinion of the accountant in regards to financial statements and schedules and in regards to the consistency of the application of the accounting principles.

Accountant's Report on Material Inadequacies, Extensions and Exemptions, Notification of Changes of Fiscal Year, and Filing Requirements

Accountant's report on material inadequacies - a supplemental report is to accompany the filing of the annual audit report that describes any material inadequacies found to exist during the audit.

Extensions and exemptions - a broker's or dealer's annual filing dates may be extended by an examining authority. Exemptions may be given to certain banks and insurance companies. The SEC has the authority to grant any extension or exemption. A broker or dealer is exempt from the Rule if he is not a member of a national securities exchange or registered national securities association.

Notification of changes of fiscal year - if a broker or dealer decides it is necessary to change his fiscal year, a notice of such must be filed with the SEC.

Filing requirements - filings are deemed to have been accomplished when they are received by the SEC.

Capital Compliance, and Regulatory Notification and Business Curtailment

Capital compliance (FINRA Rule 4110) - for the safety of public interest, FINRA may at any time impose a capital requirement that is greater than what would ordinarily be required. If a member is not compliant with capital requirements he must suspend all business operations.

Regulatory notification and business curtailment (FINRA Rule 4120) - a FINRA member is to notify FINRA within 24 hours if his capital requirement falls below certain thresholds. If a member does not meet the capital thresholds for a period of 15 days or more, it is not permitted to expand its business during this time period. A member is required to reduce his business until he meets the capital requirements.

Audit, and Notifications, Questionnaires and Reports

Audit (FINRA Rule 4140) - FINRA may at any time direct a member to have an audit completed by an independent public accountant or according to other standards.

Notifications, questionnaires and reports (FINRA Rule 4521) - a carrying or clearing member is to submit to FINRA financial and operational information regarding the member that FINRA deems essential for the protection of investors and public interest. If a member is approved to use an alternative method of computing net capital, it must file supplemental and alternative reports. A carrying or clearing member is to notify FINRA within 48 hours if his tentative net capital has declined 20% or more.

Time Within Which Margin or "Mark to Market" Must Be Obtained, Practice of Meeting Regulation T Margin Calls by Liquidation Prohibited, and Special Initial and Maintenance Margin Requirements

Time within which margin or "mark to market" must be obtained - the amount of margin or "mark to market" required must be obtained as quickly as possible, and never more than 15 business days after the deficiency date.

Practice of meeting Regulation T margin calls by liquidation prohibited - members are not to allow customers to defer the cash deposit required by a margin call or to make a practice of liquidating a commitment in the account to satisfy the call.

Special initial and maintenance margin requirements -

- FINRA reserves the right to prescribe higher initial margin requirements, higher maintenance margin requirements, and other terms and conditions.
- Special requirements for pattern day traders - the minimum margin required for a pattern day trader is $25,000, and he cannot trade in excess of his day-trading buying power, which is his equity at of the close of the previous business day, less any margin requirement.

Generally Accepted Accounting Principles (GAAP) and the Financial Accounting Standards Board (FASB)

Generally Accepted Accounting Principles (GAAP) is an internationally accepted set of accounting principles that can be incorporated in any company, locality, or country that follow the guidelines. The organization tries to impart fairness, particularly in an investor's ability to trust that a company or government's financial statements are put together using the same set of underlying rules and principles. The Financial Accounting Standards Board (FASB) is a non-profit organization based out of the United States which helps ensure that Generally Accepted Accounting Principles (GAAP) are implemented and strictly followed by all public companies in the United States.

General Ledger

A firm's general ledger is an accounting record by which records of all of the firm's transactions are kept. The general ledger is typically the source document from which reports such as financial statements originate. General ledgers also contain information about the firm's income, assets, liabilities, owners' equity, expenses, etc. Such information is very useful to an investor considering buying equity in a firm, and can be an indicator of the health of the firm.

Broker/dealers' general ledgers are subject to scrutiny by self-regulatory organizations (usually FINRA) to ensure that consumers' funds are not at risk due to poor management of the broker/dealer.

Minimum Net Capital Requirements

Minimum net capital requirements - every broker or dealer is to have a minimum net capital amount that does not allow the aggregate indebtedness to exceed 1500% of its net capital, or another minimum net capital requirement amount as specified below, whichever is greater.

- Broker-dealers who carry customer accounts - at least $250,000.
- Broker-dealers who carry accounts but do not hold customer funds or securities and operate under Paragraph (k)(2)(i) exemption of Rule 15c3-3 - at least $100,000.
- Market makers - at least $2,500 for each security for which it is a market maker.
- Dealers - at least $100,000.

Introducing Broker-Dealers

- Firms that introduce accounts on a fully disclosed basis to another broker or dealer and do not receive funds or securities - at least $5,000.
- Firms that introduce accounts on a fully disclosed basis to another broker or dealer and receive—but do not hold—customer or other broker-dealer securities and do not receive funds - at least $50,000.

Mutual fund brokers or dealers transacting a business in redeemable shares of registered investment companies and certain other share accounts - at least $25,000. A broker or dealer under this net capital requirement must promptly transmit all funds and deliver securities (on a wire order basis) and may not otherwise hold funds or securities for customers (subscription basis).

Losing a 15c3-3(k) Exemption

Approval of Change in Exempt Status under SEC Rule 15c3-3 (NASD Rule 3140) - a member can lose its 15c3-3(k) exemption when the member conducts business that will change its exempted status without the prior written approval of the NASD.

Investment Risk

Call risk is the chance that a callable bond will be called, causing the bondholder to lose the stream of interest payments left until maturity. Because bonds are generally called when interest rates are going lower, the bondholder will have a hard time getting a comparable interest rate with the money received if the bond is called. To mitigate this risk, in addition to the call premium that is paid, callable bonds usually have a call protection feature—a period of time during which the issuer may not call the bonds, usually five to ten years in duration.

Capital risk is the risk of losing all the capital one has invested, particularly for options and warrants. Such securities have expiration dates, and therefore investors can lose all their money at those dates. Purchasing investment-grade bonds can help reduce this risk.

Credit risk is the risk for a creditor that principal and interest on a loan he has given will not be paid back to him on time. Bond rating agencies (e.g. Moody's, Standard & Poor's, and Fitch) help investors to properly rate bond investments for their credit risk.

Notification Provisions for Brokers and Dealers

Notification provisions for brokers and dealers - a broker or dealer is to give notice the day of, if his net capital declines below the required minimum amount stated in Rule 15c3-1. A broker or dealer is to give notice within 24 hours if his aggregate indebtedness or net capital pass certain threshold levels detailed in the Rule. A broker or dealer is to give notice on the same day if he fails to keep current the required books and records. A broker or dealer is to give notice within 24 hours of the discovery of a material inadequacy and transmit a report within 48 hours stating what is being done to correct the situation.

Reporting Institution

Definition of reporting institution - includes every national securities exchange and its members, registered securities association, broker, dealer, municipal securities dealer, government securities broker, government securities dealer, registered transfer agent, registered clearing agency and participants, member of the Federal Reserve System, and bank with deposits insured by the FDIC.

Reporting requirements - all reporting agencies are to report to the SEC the following within 1 business day -

- The theft or loss of any securities certificates believed to be based in criminal activity;
- Any missing or lost securities certificates that have been misplaced for a period of two days and not believed to be based in criminal activity; or
- Any counterfeit securities discovered. This is also to be reported to the FBI.

Financial Recordkeeping and Reporting of Currency and Foreign Transactions

Financial recordkeeping and reporting of currency and foreign transactions (Rule 17a-8) - each registered broker or dealer subject to the Currency and Foreign Transactions Reporting Act of 1970 is to comply with the recordkeeping and record retention requirements of Chapter 10 of Title 31 of the Code of Federal Regulations. If Rule 17a-4 has requirements regarding the same records or reports but for different retention periods, the longer of the time requirements is to be kept.

Funding and Cash Management

Borrowing from or Lending to Customers

A member may borrow money from or lend money to customers if the following situations are met:

1. The member has written procedures, and
2. The customer is part of the immediate family of the borrower or lender, or
3. The customer is a financial institution regularly engaged in providing credit or loans, or
4. The customer and the registered person are both registered with the same member firm, or
5. The lending arrangement is based on a personal relationship with the customer, or
6. The lending arrangement is based on a business relationship outside the normal broker–customer relationship.

Carrying Arrangement

In general, members are not allowed to enter into an agreement to carry on an omnibus or fully disclosed basis, a customer account in which securities transactions can be made, unless the agreement is with a carrying firm that is a Financial Industry Regulatory Authority (FINRA) member. An introducing firm that acts as an intermediary for another introducing firm for purpose of obtaining clearing services from the carrying firm must notify them of the arrangement. A carrying firm may enter into carrying agreements for the carrying of customer accounts with FINRA approval. A standardized form must be used. As early as possible, no later than 10 days prior to carrying any accounts from the introducing firm, the carrying firm must send FINRA a notice introducing the firm by name and Central Registration Depository (CRD) number and include any other information specifically requested by FINRA.

A carrying arrangement must lay out the following allocations of responsibility:

1. Opening and approving of customer accounts
2. Acceptance of orders
3. Transmission of orders for execution
4. Execution of orders
5. Extension of credit
6. Receipt and delivery of funds and securities
7. Preparation and transmission of confirmations
8. Maintenance of books and records
9. Monitoring of accounts

Margin Call

A margin call is when a broker–dealer must demand that a customer deposit additional money (or securities) into an account so that the balance of the account is brought up to the minimum maintenance margin. A margin call can occur because the value of the account decreases (market fluctuations) because a withdrawal took place or because additional securities were purchased on credit. A margin call should be satisfied within 1 business period after the margin deficiency was created. If an infusion of cash or a delivery of securities is not initiated, the broker–dealer should sell securities to bring the account up to the minimum.

Special Memorandum Account (SMA)

A special memorandum account (SMA) is an account that some broker–dealers use in conjunction with a marginable account. A single entry may be used to represent both a credit to the SMA and a debit to the margin account. A payment to the customer or a transfer to another customer's account reduces the single entry amount. The SMA may contain the following entries:

1. Dividend and interest payments
2. Cash not required by this part, including cash deposited to meet maintenance margin calls
3. Proceeds of a sale of securities, or no longer required on not expired, or liquidated security position that may be withdrawn
4. Margin excess transferred from the margin account

Calculating Margin Requirements

For an equity security, 50 percent of the current market value of the security or the percentage set by the regulatory authority where the trade takes place, whichever is greater

For an exempted security, the margin requirement is the amount required by the creditor in good faith or the percentage set by the regulatory authority where the trade takes place, whichever is greater

For short sales of equity securities, the margin requirement is 150 percent of the current market value or 100 percent of the current market value if the security is convertible within 90 calendar days

For short sale of an exempted security, the margin requirement is 100 percent of the current market value of the security plus the margin required by the creditor in good faith

Short Sale

The term *short sale* refers to the sale of a security that the seller does not own or a sale that is completed by delivering a security borrowed by the seller. A customer owns a security in the following scenarios:

1. The customer (or agent) has title to it.
2. The customer has purchased it or has entered into a contract to receive it.
3. The customer owns a security that has an option to convert into it.

4. The customer has exercised an option to acquire it.
5. The customer has exercised a right or warrant to acquire it.
6. The customer owns a security features contract and received written notice that the position will be settled.

Because short sales can drive down prices, Rule 10a-1(a)(1) was enacted. It states that a listed security may be sold short at a price above the price at which the immediately preceding sale was effected (plus tick) or at the last sale price if it is higher than the last different price (zero-plus tick). Short sales are not allowed on minus ticks or zero-minus ticks. To allow exchanges to put this rule in place, the tick test was implemented. The tick test allows for unrestricted short selling (at plus tick and zero-plus ticks) while preventing short selling at successively lower prices. There are exemptions to this rule for bona-fide arbitrage, risk arbitrage, and hedge fund activities.

Situations in Which an Account Will Be Deemed to Be Exempt from Margin Requirements

An exempt account is one that falls under 1 of these categories:

1. A designated account (bank, savings association, insurance company, investment company, state or political subdivision of state, pension or profit sharing plan)
2. A person who has a net worth of at least $45 million and registered assets of at least $40 million and is either fulfilling their reporting requirements or furnishes information to the Securities & Exchange Commission (SEC)

Initial Margin Requirement

In order for a customer to purchase securities on margin, the customer is required to deposit a specific amount of margin in cash or securities. The amount must be the greater of 1 of the following:

1. The amount specifically referenced in Regulation T
2. A greater amount specified by Financial Industry Regulatory Authority (FINRA, based on the specific securities)
3. Equity of at least $2,000, except that cash does not need to be deposited in excess of the cost of any security purchased in a cash account. (The minimum for a pattern day trader is $25,000.)

MAINTENANCE MARGIN

Maintenance margin is the minimum equity that must be maintained in account in which margin is permitted. This amount is based on the type of securities held in the account:

1. 25 percent of the current market value of all margin securities, except for security future contracts that are long
2. \$2.50 per share or 100 percent of current market value (whichever is greater) for each stock short in the account selling at a price that is less than \$5
3. \$5.00 per share or 30 percent of the current market value (whichever is greater) for each stock short in the account selling at a price greater than \$5
4. 5 percent of the principal amount or 30 percent of the current market value (whichever is greater) for each short bond in the account
5. 20 percent of the current value of any security futures contracts
6. 100 percent of the current market value of each non-margin-eligible equity security

MARGIN REQUIREMENTS FOR OPTIONS (BASED ON THE UNDERLYING SECURITY)

The margin requirements for options are based on the underlying security. The following chart provides the information:

Type of Option	Initial or Maintenance Margin	Minimum Margin	Underlying Component Value
Stock	20%	10%	Equivalent number of shares at current market price
Industry index stock group	20%	10%	Index group value x applicable index multiplier
Broad index stock group	15%	10%	Index group value x applicable index multiplier
US Treasury Bills	0.35%	0.005%	The underlying principal amount
US Treasury Notes	3%	0.05%	The underlying principal amount
US Treasury Bonds	3.5%	0.05%	The underlying principal amount
Foreign Currency Options and Warrants	4%	0.75%	Units per foreign currency contract x the closing spot price
Interest Rate Contracts	10%	5%	Current interest rate measure x the applicable multiplier

Type of Option	Initial or Maintenance Margin	Minimum Margin	Underlying Component Value
Stock Index Warrant on Broad Index Stock Group	15%	10%	Index group value x the applicable index multiplier
Stock Index Warrant on Industry Index Stock Group	20%	10%	Index group value x the applicable index multiplier

Margin Requirements for Over-the-Counter (OTC) Options (Based on the Underlying Security)

The margin requirements for over-the-counter (OTC) options are based on the underlying security. The following chart provides the information:

Type of Option	Initial or Maintenance Margin	Min. Margin	Underlying Component Value
Stock and Convertible Corporate Debt Securities	30%	10%	Equivalent number of shares at current market price
Industry Index Stock Group	30%	10%	Index group value x the applicable index multiplier
Broad Index Stock Group	20%	10%	Index group value x the applicable index multiplier
US Government or US Government Agency Debt Securities	5%	3%	The underlying principal amount
Listed Non-Equity Securities	15%	5%	The underlying principal amount
All Other OTC Options	45%	20%	The underlying principal amount

How to Overcome Test Anxiety

Just the thought of taking a test is enough to make most people a little nervous. A test is an important event that can have a long-term impact on your future, so it's important to take it seriously and it's natural to feel anxious about performing well. But just because anxiety is normal, that doesn't mean that it's helpful in test taking, or that you should simply accept it as part of your life. Anxiety can have a variety of effects. These effects can be mild, like making you feel slightly nervous, or severe, like blocking your ability to focus or remember even a simple detail.

If you experience test anxiety—whether severe or mild—it's important to know how to beat it. To discover this, first you need to understand what causes test anxiety.

Causes of Test Anxiety

While we often think of anxiety as an uncontrollable emotional state, it can actually be caused by simple, practical things. One of the most common causes of test anxiety is that a person does not feel adequately prepared for their test. This feeling can be the result of many different issues such as poor study habits or lack of organization, but the most common culprit is time management. Starting to study too late, failing to organize your study time to cover all of the material, or being distracted while you study will mean that you're not well prepared for the test. This may lead to cramming the night before, which will cause you to be physically and mentally exhausted for the test. Poor time management also contributes to feelings of stress, fear, and hopelessness as you realize you are not well prepared but don't know what to do about it.

Other times, test anxiety is not related to your preparation for the test but comes from unresolved fear. This may be a past failure on a test, or poor performance on tests in general. It may come from comparing yourself to others who seem to be performing better or from the stress of living up to expectations. Anxiety may be driven by fears of the future—how failure on this test would affect your educational and career goals. These fears are often completely irrational, but they can still negatively impact your test performance.

Elements of Test Anxiety

As mentioned earlier, test anxiety is considered to be an emotional state, but it has physical and mental components as well. Sometimes you may not even realize that you are suffering from test anxiety until you notice the physical symptoms. These can include trembling hands, rapid heartbeat, sweating, nausea, and tense muscles. Extreme anxiety may lead to fainting or vomiting. Obviously, any of these symptoms can have a negative impact on testing. It is important to recognize them as soon as they begin to occur so that you can address the problem before it damages your performance.

The mental components of test anxiety include trouble focusing and inability to remember learned information. During a test, your mind is on high alert, which can help you recall information and stay focused for an extended period of time. However, anxiety interferes with your mind's natural processes, causing you to blank out, even on the questions you know well. The strain of testing during anxiety makes it difficult to stay focused, especially on a test that may take several hours. Extreme anxiety can take a huge mental toll, making it difficult not only to recall test information but even to understand the test questions or pull your thoughts together.

Effects of Test Anxiety

Test anxiety is like a disease—if left untreated, it will get progressively worse. Anxiety leads to poor performance, and this reinforces the feelings of fear and failure, which in turn lead to poor performances on subsequent tests. It can grow from a mild nervousness to a crippling condition. If allowed to progress, test anxiety can have a big impact on your schooling, and consequently on your future.

Test anxiety can spread to other parts of your life. Anxiety on tests can become anxiety in any stressful situation, and blanking on a test can turn into panicking in a job situation. But fortunately, you don't have to let anxiety rule your testing and determine your grades. There are a number of relatively simple steps you can take to move past anxiety and function normally on a test and in the rest of life.

Physical Steps for Beating Test Anxiety

While test anxiety is a serious problem, the good news is that it can be overcome. It doesn't have to control your ability to think and remember information. While it may take time, you can begin taking steps today to beat anxiety.

Just as your first hint that you may be struggling with anxiety comes from the physical symptoms, the first step to treating it is also physical. Rest is crucial for having a clear, strong mind. If you are tired, it is much easier to give in to anxiety. But if you establish good sleep habits, your body and mind will be ready to perform optimally, without the strain of exhaustion. Additionally, sleeping well helps you to retain information better, so you're more likely to recall the answers when you see the test questions.

Getting good sleep means more than going to bed on time. It's important to allow your brain time to relax. Take study breaks from time to time so it doesn't get overworked, and don't study right before bed. Take time to rest your mind before trying to rest your body, or you may find it difficult to fall asleep.

Along with sleep, other aspects of physical health are important in preparing for a test. Good nutrition is vital for good brain function. Sugary foods and drinks may give a burst of energy but this burst is followed by a crash, both physically and emotionally. Instead, fuel your body with protein and vitamin-rich foods.

Also, drink plenty of water. Dehydration can lead to headaches and exhaustion, especially if your brain is already under stress from the rigors of the test. Particularly if your test is a long one, drink water during the breaks. And if possible, take an energy-boosting snack to eat between sections.

Along with sleep and diet, a third important part of physical health is exercise. Maintaining a steady workout schedule is helpful, but even taking 5-minute study breaks to walk can help get your blood pumping faster and clear your head. Exercise also releases endorphins, which contribute to a positive feeling and can help combat test anxiety.

When you nurture your physical health, you are also contributing to your mental health. If your body is healthy, your mind is much more likely to be healthy as well. So take time to rest, nourish your body with healthy food and water, and get moving as much as possible. Taking these physical steps will make you stronger and more able to take the mental steps necessary to overcome test anxiety.

Mental Steps for Beating Test Anxiety

Working on the mental side of test anxiety can be more challenging, but as with the physical side, there are clear steps you can take to overcome it. As mentioned earlier, test anxiety often stems from lack of preparation, so the obvious solution is to prepare for the test. Effective studying may be the most important weapon you have for beating test anxiety, but you can and should employ several other mental tools to combat fear.

First, boost your confidence by reminding yourself of past success—tests or projects that you aced. If you're putting as much effort into preparing for this test as you did for those, there's no reason you should expect to fail here. Work hard to prepare; then trust your preparation.

Second, surround yourself with encouraging people. It can be helpful to find a study group, but be sure that the people you're around will encourage a positive attitude. If you spend time with others who are anxious or cynical, this will only contribute to your own anxiety. Look for others who are motivated to study hard from a desire to succeed, not from a fear of failure.

Third, reward yourself. A test is physically and mentally tiring, even without anxiety, and it can be helpful to have something to look forward to. Plan an activity following the test, regardless of the outcome, such as going to a movie or getting ice cream.

When you are taking the test, if you find yourself beginning to feel anxious, remind yourself that you know the material. Visualize successfully completing the test. Then take a few deep, relaxing breaths and return to it. Work through the questions carefully but with confidence, knowing that you are capable of succeeding.

Developing a healthy mental approach to test taking will also aid in other areas of life. Test anxiety affects more than just the actual test—it can be damaging to your mental health and even contribute to depression. It's important to beat test anxiety before it becomes a problem for more than testing.

Study Strategy

Being prepared for the test is necessary to combat anxiety, but what does being prepared look like? You may study for hours on end and still not feel prepared. What you need is a strategy for test prep. The next few pages outline our recommended steps to help you plan out and conquer the challenge of preparation.

Step 1: Scope Out the Test

Learn everything you can about the format (multiple choice, essay, etc.) and what will be on the test. Gather any study materials, course outlines, or sample exams that may be available. Not only will this help you to prepare, but knowing what to expect can help to alleviate test anxiety.

Step 2: Map Out the Material

Look through the textbook or study guide and make note of how many chapters or sections it has. Then divide these over the time you have. For example, if a book has 15 chapters and you have five days to study, you need to cover three chapters each day. Even better, if you have the time, leave an extra day at the end for overall review after you have gone through the material in depth.

If time is limited, you may need to prioritize the material. Look through it and make note of which sections you think you already have a good grasp on, and which need review. While you are studying, skim quickly through the familiar sections and take more time on the challenging parts. Write out your plan so you don't get lost as you go. Having a written plan also helps you feel more in control of the study, so anxiety is less likely to arise from feeling overwhelmed at the amount to cover.

Step 3: Gather Your Tools

Decide what study method works best for you. Do you prefer to highlight in the book as you study and then go back over the highlighted portions? Or do you type out notes of the important information? Or is it helpful to make flashcards that you can carry with you? Assemble the pens, index cards, highlighters, post-it notes, and any other materials you may need so you won't be distracted by getting up to find things while you study.

If you're having a hard time retaining the information or organizing your notes, experiment with different methods. For example, try color-coding by subject with colored pens, highlighters, or post-it notes. If you learn better by hearing, try recording yourself reading your notes so you can listen while in the car, working out, or simply sitting at your desk. Ask a friend to quiz you from your flashcards, or try teaching someone the material to solidify it in your mind.

STEP 4: CREATE YOUR ENVIRONMENT

It's important to avoid distractions while you study. This includes both the obvious distractions like visitors and the subtle distractions like an uncomfortable chair (or a too-comfortable couch that makes you want to fall asleep). Set up the best study environment possible: good lighting and a comfortable work area. If background music helps you focus, you may want to turn it on, but otherwise keep the room quiet. If you are using a computer to take notes, be sure you don't have any other windows open, especially applications like social media, games, or anything else that could distract you. Silence your phone and turn off notifications. Be sure to keep water close by so you stay hydrated while you study (but avoid unhealthy drinks and snacks).

Also, take into account the best time of day to study. Are you freshest first thing in the morning? Try to set aside some time then to work through the material. Is your mind clearer in the afternoon or evening? Schedule your study session then. Another method is to study at the same time of day that you will take the test, so that your brain gets used to working on the material at that time and will be ready to focus at test time.

STEP 5: STUDY!

Once you have done all the study preparation, it's time to settle into the actual studying. Sit down, take a few moments to settle your mind so you can focus, and begin to follow your study plan. Don't give in to distractions or let yourself procrastinate. This is your time to prepare so you'll be ready to fearlessly approach the test. Make the most of the time and stay focused.

Of course, you don't want to burn out. If you study too long you may find that you're not retaining the information very well. Take regular study breaks. For example, taking five minutes out of every hour to walk briskly, breathing deeply and swinging your arms, can help your mind stay fresh.

As you get to the end of each chapter or section, it's a good idea to do a quick review. Remind yourself of what you learned and work on any difficult parts. When you feel that you've mastered the material, move on to the next part. At the end of your study session, briefly skim through your notes again.

But while review is helpful, cramming last minute is NOT. If at all possible, work ahead so that you won't need to fit all your study into the last day. Cramming overloads your brain with more information than it can process and retain, and your tired mind may struggle to recall even previously learned information when it is overwhelmed with last-minute study. Also, the urgent nature of cramming and the stress placed on your brain contribute to anxiety. You'll be more likely to go to the test feeling unprepared and having trouble thinking clearly.

So don't cram, and don't stay up late before the test, even just to review your notes at a leisurely pace. Your brain needs rest more than it needs to go over the information again. In fact, plan to finish your studies by noon or early afternoon the day before the test. Give your brain the rest of the day to relax or focus on other things, and get a good night's sleep. Then you will be fresh for the test and better able to recall what you've studied.

Step 6: Take a Practice Test

Many courses offer sample tests, either online or in the study materials. This is an excellent resource to check whether you have mastered the material, as well as to prepare for the test format and environment.

Check the test format ahead of time: the number of questions, the type (multiple choice, free response, etc.), and the time limit. Then create a plan for working through them. For example, if you have 30 minutes to take a 60-question test, your limit is 30 seconds per question. Spend less time on the questions you know well so that you can take more time on the difficult ones.

If you have time to take several practice tests, take the first one open book, with no time limit. Work through the questions at your own pace and make sure you fully understand them. Gradually work up to taking a test under test conditions: sit at a desk with all study materials put away and set a timer. Pace yourself to make sure you finish the test with time to spare and go back to check your answers if you have time.

After each test, check your answers. On the questions you missed, be sure you understand why you missed them. Did you misread the question (tests can use tricky wording)? Did you forget the information? Or was it something you hadn't learned? Go back and study any shaky areas that the practice tests reveal.

Taking these tests not only helps with your grade, but also aids in combating test anxiety. If you're already used to the test conditions, you're less likely to worry about it, and working through tests until you're scoring well gives you a confidence boost. Go through the practice tests until you feel comfortable, and then you can go into the test knowing that you're ready for it.

Test Tips

On test day, you should be confident, knowing that you've prepared well and are ready to answer the questions. But aside from preparation, there are several test day strategies you can employ to maximize your performance.

First, as stated before, get a good night's sleep the night before the test (and for several nights before that, if possible). Go into the test with a fresh, alert mind rather than staying up late to study.

Try not to change too much about your normal routine on the day of the test. It's important to eat a nutritious breakfast, but if you normally don't eat breakfast at all, consider eating just a protein bar. If you're a coffee drinker, go ahead and have your normal coffee. Just make sure you time it so that the caffeine doesn't wear off right in the middle of your test. Avoid sugary beverages, and drink enough water to stay hydrated but not so much that you need a restroom break 10 minutes into the test. If your test isn't first thing in the morning, consider going for a walk or doing a light workout before the test to get your blood flowing.

Allow yourself enough time to get ready, and leave for the test with plenty of time to spare so you won't have the anxiety of scrambling to arrive in time. Another reason to be early is to select a good seat. It's helpful to sit away from doors and windows, which can be distracting. Find a good seat, get out your supplies, and settle your mind before the test begins.

When the test begins, start by going over the instructions carefully, even if you already know what to expect. Make sure you avoid any careless mistakes by following the directions.

Then begin working through the questions, pacing yourself as you've practiced. If you're not sure on an answer, don't spend too much time on it, and don't let it shake your confidence. Either skip it and come back later, or eliminate as many wrong answers as possible and guess among the remaining ones. Don't dwell on these questions as you continue—put them out of your mind and focus on what lies ahead.

Be sure to read all of the answer choices, even if you're sure the first one is the right answer. Sometimes you'll find a better one if you keep reading. But don't second-guess yourself if you do immediately know the answer. Your gut instinct is usually right. Don't let test anxiety rob you of the information you know.

If you have time at the end of the test (and if the test format allows), go back and review your answers. Be cautious about changing any, since your first instinct tends to be correct, but make sure you didn't misread any of the questions or accidentally mark the wrong answer choice. Look over any you skipped and make an educated guess.

At the end, leave the test feeling confident. You've done your best, so don't waste time worrying about your performance or wishing you could change anything. Instead, celebrate the successful completion of this test. And finally, use this test to learn how to deal with anxiety even better next time.

Review Video: Test Anxiety
Visit mometrix.com/academy and enter code: 100340

Important Qualification

Not all anxiety is created equal. If your test anxiety is causing major issues in your life beyond the classroom or testing center, or if you are experiencing troubling physical symptoms related to your anxiety, it may be a sign of a serious physiological or psychological condition. If this sounds like your situation, we strongly encourage you to seek professional help.

Online Resources

Due to our efforts to try to keep this book to a manageable length, we've created a link that will give you access to all of your online resources:

mometrix.com/resources719/series27

It's Your Moment, Let's Celebrate It!

Share your story @mometrixtestpreparation